PEACE
New Method, New Light

Olivier Manitara

PEACE

New Method, New Light

Telesma-Evida Publishing

I dedicate this book to all those who pass upon the earth and carry in their souls the light of a high ideal for the good and the welfare of all beings.

May we, one day, be able to celebrate the loving alliance of all men, beyond all boundaries, and unite our forces for the healthy and harmonious development of humanity and of the earth.

Olivier Manitara

PEACE–NEW METHOD, NEW LIGHT
Copyright © 1999 by Telesma-Evida Publishing Inc.
All rights reserved worldwide.
No part of this book may be reproduced or transmitted in any form or by any means, electronic or mechanical, including photocopying, recording, or by any information storage and retrieval system, without written permission from the publisher, except in the case of quotations embodied in critical articles and reviews.

Canadian Cataloguing in Publication Data

Manitara, Olivier, 1964-
   Peace : new method, new light

Translation of: La paix.
Includes bibliographical references.
ISBN 1-894341-01-5

  1. Peace of mind. 2. Peace. I. Title.

B105.P4M3513 1999   158.1   C99-900231-7

Legal deposit first quarter 1999
National Library of Canada
National Library of Quebec

Printed in Canada on acid-free paper

CONTENTS

I Am You, 15

The Kingdom of Peace Is Like a Hen, 17

Chapter 1—The Manual of Peace, 19
    Respect—A Key For Peace, 20
    Peace Is A Cake, 21

The Kingdom of Peace Is Like a King, 23

Chapter 2—The Mystery of the Two Kinds of Peace, 25
    The Practical Value Of The Teaching Of Christ, 25
    The Awakening Of The Consciousness To The Art Of Combat, 27
    The Secrets Of The Pentagram: White Magic And Black Magic, 29
    It Is Impossible To Achieve Peace Without Transforming Oneself, 34
    Do Not Allow Yourself To Be Enslaved By Fear, 35
    Mastering The Fire Of Love, 36
    Handling The Sword Of Decisions, 38

The Negative Being Makes Everything Harmful; The Positive Being Makes Everything Beneficial, 40

The Work Of The Masters, 42

The Five Stages On The Path Of Peace, 44

The Healing Of The Being Of War, 49

To Be Or Not To Be—That Is The Question, 51

The Accumulation Of Discontentment—The Source Of War, 52

The Image And The Influence Of The Devil, 54

Peace Resides Beyond The Illusory Appearances, 56

The Paths Of The Two Kinds Of Peace, 58

The Technique Of Harmony And Of Cosmic Unification, 59

The Peace That The World Does Not Know, 62

The Person Who Wants To Keep His Illusions Is Not Ready For Peace, 63

Peace Is Not A Box Of Sleeping Pills, 64

God Has No Side: He Is Indivisible, 66

The Kingdom of Peace Is Like a Village, 69

Chapter 3—The Great Meditation: the Tree of Peace, 71

The Double-Edged Sword Of The Archangel Michael, 71

Exercise of the Internal Awakening of the Consciousness, 73

Introduce The Light Of The Spirit Into Everything You Do, 75

The Spirit Is Perfect And Matter Is Perfectible, 77

The Unity Of The Spirit, 79

The Balance Between The Spiritual Life And The Material Life, 80

The Universal Key Of Peace: The Great Method, 81

Become Aware Of The Ground Which Carries You, 83

Above You: The Immensity Of The Sky, 85

Words Of Light On The Law Of Evolution, 87

The Great Secret Of Initiation And Peace, 89

The Great Meditation For Peace: The Ground, You, And The Sky, 90

The Great Meditation For Peace: Life, 92

The Great Meditation: The Purification Of Desire, 93

The Great Meditation: The Force Of The Will And The Miracle Of The Person, 97

The Great Meditation: The Elevation Of The Heart, 101

The Great Meditation: The Mastery Of The Thoughts, 106

The Great Meditation: The Eternal "I", 107

The Great Meditation: The Original Gnosis And The Land Of Light, 108

The Great Meditation: The Omnipresence Of The Holy Spirit, 110

The Great Meditation: The Force Of The Holy Spirit Is The Only Force, 111

The Great Meditation: The Unmanifested, 116

The Living Tradition, 119

The Tree of Peace, 120

Chapter 4—The Response of the Eternal, 127

The Kingdom of Peace Is Like an Emigrant, 129

Chapter 5—The Consciousness of Exchanges: a Key for Peace, 131

    The Communion With The Universe, 131

    The Two Paths Of The Consciousness, 133

    The Experiment In A Public Park, 134

    A Disciple Must Unite Himself With The Sublime Spirit Which Soars Above Creation, 136

    The Disciple's Experience With A Master-Tree, 138

    The Energy of Evil Is All the More Dangerous When It Is Invisible, 140

    No Act Is Insignificant, 141

    No One Else Can Be Conscious For You, 143

    Without Purity, Peace Is Impossible, 145

    The Truth Is Inside Of You, 148

    Everything Is Magical, 148

The Kingdom of Peace Is Like a Woman, 151

Chapter 6—I Am Gentle and Humble of Heart, 153

Chapter 7—The Three Keys, 159

Chapter 8—Vegetarianism for Peace, 161

Chapter 9—Words for Awakened Men, 165

Chapter 10—The Heroic Path of Shamballa, 167

    History Is Always Repeating Itself, 167

    Put The Will Of The Most High Above Everything Else, 169

    The Idea Of A Humanity Of Light, 171

    The Land Of Light Of The Guides Of Humanity, 172

    The Consecration To The Archangel Michael, 173

    Humanity In The Clutches Of The Dragon, 176

    The Art Of The Fight Which Saves, 178

The Kingdom of Peace Is Like Pure Water, 181

Chapter 11—The Egregor of the Dove and the Triumph of Free Peace, 183

    The Free And Creative Man, 183

    The Egregor Of The Dove: Source of The True Peace, 186

    The Art Of Creating Gods, 187

    The Thursday Ceremony Of The Students Of The School of St. John, 188

    The Mystery Of The Egregors, 192

The Kingdom of Peace Is Like a Person Who Is Walking, 197

Chapter 12—The Truth Does Not Ask Your Opinion, 201

The Kingdom of Peace Is Like a Flowing Spring, 205

Chapter 13—Thursday's Circle Of Peace, 207

The Kingdom of Peace Is Like a Mother, 211

Chapter 14—The Origin of Wars, 215

The Kingdom of Peace Is Like a Chemist, 217

Chapter 15—The Will of the Most High, 219

The Kingdom of Peace Is Like a Gardener, 221

About the Author, 225

I Am You

I Am you, I who speak to you,
I Am your life—the source of life,
I Am your strength—the source of strength,
I Am your elevation—the source of elevation,
I Am your joy—the source of happiness,
I Am your wisdom—the source of wisdom,
I Am your destiny—the source of every path,
I Am your love—the source of love,
I Am your fulfillment—the source of plenitude,
I Am your peace—the source of spiritual unity.
So have confidence in me, the spirit of the I-Am sun,
and I will guide you towards the kingdom of peace.

Cosmic Tradition
School of St. John

THE KINGDOM OF PEACE IS LIKE A HEN

The kingdom of peace is like a hen pecking at grains of wheat in a field. Suddenly she finds a large diamond—but, taking it for a miserable pebble, she rejects it with disdain.

In truth, I say to you: with this diamond, the hen could have bought the finest wheat, and even the farm, and could have become the employer of the farmer, the man who thinks only of fattening her up—all the better to devour her.

THE MANUAL OF PEACE

Dear reader, you who are seeking pearls of truth upon the path of life, know that, for me, peace is not a human invention—something manufactured and artificial—but, truly, a vibration which does not come from the earth.

That is why this manual of peace wants to guide you towards a higher reality and perception of yourself and of the world. Then, a light of knowledge and of a higher life will appear inside you, and will reveal to you the kingdom of your soul and the land of true peace. If we carefully study the history of humanity, we notice very quickly that many people have come to know cosmic peace and have merged with it. Their lives were transformed and enlarged; and, in a natural way, they began to radiate peace, joy and healing all around them, and became benefactors to humanity. They all told us that there was a path for attaining peace, and they associated this peace with the highest knowledge that man can attain on the earth—the knowledge of Oneself and of the Supreme One.

Obviously, this is a mystical quest—and, therefore, internal, essential and vital.

Authentic peace opens up the knowledge of the eternal soul; it resides beyond even the boundaries of death and of lust. Without its presence, man passes through this world like a shadow, ignorant of the beautiful light that lives inside of him, and of the light from which he draws his origin.

Respect—A Key For Peace

Thus, the words gathered together and united in this manual do not come from a man and do not belong to anyone—even though many people, throughout time, have spoken them and have merged with them.

Peace does not belong to anyone; it belongs to itself.

Man must not monopolize peace for the satisfaction of his personal needs; on the contrary, he must truly recognize the supremacy of the being of peace, respect it, bow before it, and put himself at its service.

To respect oneself is to respect what is above oneself, as well as what is below oneself, while recognizing the unity of creation, of life and of the consciousness.

The man who is awakened from the inside, who respects himself, will not be able to prostitute peace, nor to degrade any being, because he knows that everything is alive and aware of the same life and consciousness that is living inside of him. Forms and appearances are many and different; for example, peace is an idea that has no body and is not designed like a man. But that is not important; it is simply another manifestation of life—just like stones, insects, etc.

The person who, in a healthy way, respects his human nature, and the life and consciousness living inside of him, will discover that he admires the entire universe and that he is entering into the teaching of the sacred mysteries. He comes to life; he truly becomes a man.

Peace Is A Cake

These words emanate from the one-source of the cosmic wisdom which flows eternally to quench the thirst of those who love life.

They resound through every soul, and their echo can awaken the inner life and lead the person who knows how to listen to them in silence onto the path of true peace.

A manual is not meant just to be read; instead, it invites one to the actual practice, and it conveys a certain know-how. In order to taste the cake of peace, one has to put one's hands into the dough. No one will build peace in your place. Yes, peace is a cake composed of a multitude of ingredients, which one has to know how to unite harmoniously, according to a precise art. Many people have looked for peace without success precisely because they did not understand this law. Peace is a state of being which appears all by itself when all of the necessary conditions are brought together.

It is not only a cake, but also the cherry on top of the cake. The words in this manual are the ingredients; and that is why you must invite them into yourself with purity, awareness and patience, carefully meditate upon them, fill yourself up with them, taste them, nourish yourself with them, breathe them in, and become one with them.

Then they will open up the inner door of the man who is worthy, noble and good; of the luminous, just, awakened man; of the artisan of peace.

These words contain a vibration which can transform life, ennoble it and rejuvenate it, and which can lead one onto the true path of free peace.

Blessed are the ardent ones who commit themselves to this path of peace, for they will find the treasure of light of their souls.

THE KINGDOM OF PEACE IS LIKE A KING

The kingdom of peace is like a king who raises an army to go off to war. He wins all of the battles, and the victory is his. He is filled with joy because he has crushed his enemies. But he soon realizes that many of his best friends are dead; and he sees, once again, the faces of those he has killed, with their blood still staining his armor. He says to himself: "Do they, perhaps, have wives and children weeping for them now?"

His heart becomes filled with sadness; he knows that the real enemy has not been defeated.

In truth, I say to you, there is never any victory in external wars. It is always man who loses. It is impossible to separate victory and defeat in this kind of war.

The real enemy is inside oneself; the person who triumphs over it elevates himself above that victory-defeat, to find the light of the kingdom that I am telling you about.

THE MYSTERY OF THE TWO KINDS OF PEACE

The Practical Value Of The Teaching Of Christ

Jesus said: *"Human beings may think that I have come to bring peace into the world; they do not know that I have come to sow division on the earth—fire, the sword, war. Because, where there are five in one house, three will be against two and two against three—the father against the son, the son against the father; they will all stand alone."*

These words, coming from the mouth of Christ, are truly strange, because how could the one who is pure love, goodness and wisdom—the one who bestowed his peace on his disciples as he left them—say that he came to sow war in the world?

Christ is a being of peace; he is its symbol, incarnated in a man. When St. Peter strikes with his sword the enemy who has come to arrest the Master, he tells him: *"All those who take up the sword will die by the sword"*; and he heals the high priest's assistant. He prevents the consequences of this negative action from falling back upon his disciple, by repairing the error.

This apparent contradiction in Christ's teaching is not really one at all, because he wanted to point out to his disciples the true keys for finding peace; this is a difficult thing to teach, because human beings think that they already know what peace is— whereas Christ speaks of a peace which is not of this world, but which draws its origin from the kingdom of the spirit.

It is sad to see the extent to which those who call themselves the disciples of Christ no longer understand the meaning of his words; to make things worse, they diminish the value of this sublime teaching. The Christ who came to awaken man and to lead him into the light of his highest being finds himself transformed into a powerful soporific of the spirit, the soul and the body.

His words have become a gentle lullaby, which we listen to as we are falling asleep.

In reality, his teaching contains an extremely profound science which can transform everything inside of man and lead him onto the path of a more luminous understanding and life. For this, one must learn the art of bringing new life to these words, by meditating upon them and by assimilating their secret essence.

If you really want to advance and benefit from the teaching of Christ, it must not remain a dead message; instead, your spirit must go out to meet it, in order to bring it to life. It must become part of your daily life; and then you will discover its practical value.

The Awakening Of The Consciousness To The Art Of Combat

Christ, the champion of peace, invites his disciples to wield the sword. Not against the world or other people—which is too easy—but against themselves. This involves awakening from the inside, and becoming aware of oneself, of one's life, of one's actions, of one's path.

The first step towards peace lies in the awakening of one's own consciousness to the light of life; this awakening requires all of the ardor, the strength and the courage of a warrior who is going into combat. (1)

The awakening of the consciousness is a virtue which goes in the direction of life, while the degradation of the consciousness leads not only to death but also to the dehumanization of man.

The man who loses his consciousness and his dignity as a human being can become a monster and commit inhuman acts—but the opposite can never happen. The person who progresses in the awakening of his consciousness can't help but walk in the footsteps of Christ and of all of the great heros of humanity.

---

(1) Consult this work by the same author: "Concentration, Attention, Awakening—*Their Application in Life*". (Editor's Note.)

Human beings now do more and more things mechanically—without thinking, without awakening, without being alive. They think, eat, sleep, go to church, get dressed, work, and so on, unconsciously, without understanding the deeper meaning of all of this. These bad habits are extremely dangerous because they lead to the degradation and degeneration of the consciousness, and are also open doors for the enemies of humanity.

Human beings are so fast asleep that they no longer see the enemy coming—the one who is going to steal everything, ruin everything, destroy everything inside of them. This is why Christ recommends the art of combat—because it has become a necessity to be vigilant, focused and prepared.

Therefore, a man worthy of this name should not agree to believe in a religion whose words he does not understand, to wear garments or jewelry without knowing their significance, or to perform certain acts without grasping their deeper meaning.

Everything that we do that is not <u>vivified</u> by the spirit of awakening leads us towards death and the degeneration of the soul. Every action, every thought, every habit must become like a piece of royal armor, and must be tied to a higher idea, thought, virtue or cause. In this way, everything is tied together, everything is consecrated, everything becomes alive. Otherwise, man attracts to himself, without knowing it, the influences which will lead him to his own downfall; and peace becomes impossible to achieve.

Therefore, Christ makes each person face his own responsibilities, and says clearly that he has come to bring division—that is, a choice, a sword of decisions.

1. To bring to life; animate

World English Dictionary

This division makes it possible to separate the two paths—the path of life and awakening, and the path of death and unconsciousness.

Every man will be committed to one of these two paths—and will find himself serving, consciously, the forces of light, or, unconsciously, the forces of darkness.

The choice belongs to each person.

This is not about calling oneself a Christian or a servant of good; one must act like a Christian, like a servant of good.

The Secrets Of The Pentagram: White Magic And Black Magic

Christ puts man, the individual, at the center of his teaching on peace. Peace cannot come from the outside, nor from another person; it must be achieved by each individual, who, uniting himself fraternally with others around a common ideal, can then make it a reality on the outside.

He says: *"Where there are five in one house, three will be against two and two against three..."*; this refers to the five senses—and the house is the human being. Here, he is alluding to the flaming star which guides the wise men to him, the luminous pentagram, the five-pointed star—each point inscribed with one of the five letters in the name of Jesus; it contains, in its secret symbolism, a whole section of the teaching of the wise men, disciples of Zoroastre—the golden star.

The pentagram represents the man of light, the Christ-man, the standing man, the man ready to work for peace.

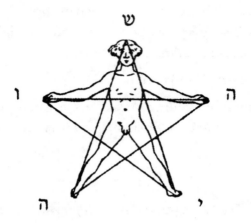

This symbol, drawn in this way, has a great and beneficial influence on the invisible light which surrounds us and in which we move and have our existence—the same influence that Christ, or any man of great goodness and wisdom, exercises all around himself.

In talking about the three against the two, Christ points out a great secret. Indeed, when the three points of the head and the arms are directed upwards, man is inside the light of his being, and he balances all of the negative forces and influences so widespread throughout the soul of the world. He is an agent of peace, in a natural way, through the equilibrium and harmony which emanate from him.

When the two points of the feet are turned upwards, then the pentagram is inverted, and one can see in it the image of the head of the goat—with its two horns, its ears and its beard. This is the sign of black magic, of false peace, of the triumph of instinctive force over intelligence, of passion over the will, of fate over liberty, of disorder over order, of unconsciousness over free consciousness.

When man forms the inverted pentagram inside himself, he then projects, all around himself, influences of illness, of lawlessness, of imbalance and of war, which disrupt the forces of the living nature and all beings. (1)

This is the teaching that Christ wanted to convey to us about peace.

There are, in fact, two kinds of peace and two humanities. One which is dominated by instinct, and the other by the light of the true intelligence which is none other than the Holy Spirit. These two humanities come face-to-face inside each individual. In the son, the Father must be fulfilled; but, in the Father, the son must also become real. Each person must find his own being, his reality, and embody it. The path of the luminous pentagram requires strength and working on oneself, while that of the dark pentagram demands no effort at all; all one has to do is to let things go their own way.

When the star is inverted in man, he naturally becomes a servant of the false peace, of the suffering humanity, of death. From him emanate, in an unconscious way, influences of fear, nastiness, injustice, slander, unconsciousness, lies, and so on.

---

(1) For a deeper, practical study of the two pentagrams, see the teachings-by-correspondence of the School of Life and Spirit.

When the pentagram is turned rightside-up again, then it is goodness, justice, love, wisdom, truth, liberty, joy and simplicity which emanate from the individual and which build peace.

This is why Christ said: *"Blessed are the artisans of peace, for they shall be called sons of God."* Since Christ himself was a son of God, this means that they will be called the same thing as him; their names will be inscribed in the pentagram of light.

In the light of these explanations, look at the world and humanity in a new way, and you will discover many things. In life, everything is a question of your point of view, of the way you look at it. The invisible can appear to the person who, quite simply, knows how to look at things in a different way.

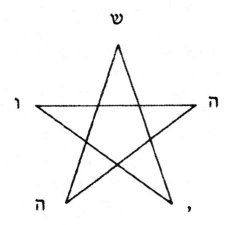

For example, how can one explain the fact that all human beings—whoever they may be—talk about, wish for and vote for peace, and that, even so, there have never been so many wars on earth? Anarchy, idiocy, injustice and dishonesty triumph on every level—everyone knows this; and humanity no longer reacts when faced with the absurd and the inhuman—having become accustomed to this disorder and to this spiritual and cultural poverty, and having given up the fight long ago with passive resignation. This is the signature of the inverted pentagram: man gives up his humanity, his intelligence and his will, in favor of the blind force which leads him where he doesn't want to go.

Where is man's dignity? In the pentagram of light! Man stands upon the earth—conscious, awakened, ready to work for the good of all beings, in full possession of all of his faculties, dominating the four elements by the light of his intelligence, which is united with the Holy Spirit and with all of the beneficent forces of the superior worlds.

Where is man's downfall? In the inverted pentagram! Man gives up his intelligence, his being, his soul and his liberty, to be dominated and enslaved by all of the wild instinctive forces—by lies, jealousy, anger, fear, selfishness, etc. He becomes an unconscious agent of evil, of destruction and hatred.

No one is immune from this; and that is why Christ says that he did not come to lull people to sleep inside a false, illusory peace which leads to death, but to bring about a free inner awakening, a reformation of the consciousness and of life, a salutary revolution.

It Is Impossible To Achieve Peace Without Transforming Oneself

This is the cause of all wars, illnesses and destruction: human beings want peace but do nothing for it—they make no effort at all. Those who take action do so to serve their own personal, selfish interests—which are dominated by instinct; but they have not awakened inside the vibration of peace which does not come from this world. That kind of peace, they think, can't bring them anything; they won't be able to sell it. Thus, what they want is not peace but the death of the spirit.

They consider peace as a means to achieve their own selfish and materialistic objectives, whereas peace, in its essence, is a sacred and unchangeable goal—a lofty destination for man. It is impossible to approach peace without transforming oneself; doing so shows an obvious lack of respect.

Peace is the summit of the highest mountain of the spirit. In order to reach it, the whole individual must be elevated and ennobled in the light.

A path of ascension for humanity, and not the possibility to do just-anything. Without order, without rules and discipline, there can be no true peace, and this order, these rules and this discipline have existed since the beginning of time; unchangeable, cosmic and eternal, they have taken many names—like the order of Melchizedek or the School of St. John. But names are nothing more than labels; the most important thing is the order itself in its primary source, and it is towards this that every man who is sincerely looking for peace must turn.

Do Not Allow Yourself To Be Enslaved By Fear

Thus, in order to find peace, you must not remain confined to your own little person, to your own petty viewpoints and interests; you must not be selfish—that is, locked up inside a small part of yourself—but, instead, open up your heart and expand your soul, learn to merge with the Whole, to taste the harmony of the worlds, to love all beings and to commune with them in spirit. Human beings no longer know how to live outside of their mortal selves—in the immensity of space, in immortality. Yet, there is nothing more beautiful than a soul taking flight towards infinity in order to taste the sacred joy and the fulfillment of the spirit. Why condemn yourself to life in a narrow, limited atmosphere—deprived of love, of exchanges in beauty, of wisdom, of purity? It is this kind of imprisonment that generates aggressiveness, hatred and violence. Abominable experiments of this type have been physically conducted on rats, which were locked up in a space that was too small—and which ended up devouring one another.

Human beings lock themselves up inside their physical bodies, inside their ephemeral personalities, inside their shrivelled-up little egos—rejecting the whole spiritual part of their being. They want to have experiences only below, within the body—never above, within the free spirit. This is why they are afraid of death, afraid of everything—dominated by fear.

The person who is in harmony with himself does not let fear dominate his life. A life dominated by fear—fear of dying, of living, of failing, of succeeding—is not a life, but a death in disguise. In the same way, peace inspired by fear, by the instinctive forces, is not peace, but a travesty which can only generate catastrophes.

Whatever the path that he takes at any given moment, the individual is always alone with himself. No amount of fear, no amount of running away, can erase this fact. At the moment of death, man finds himself alone with himself. No one can replace him in this experience; there is no possible escape.

This solitude is an initiatic experience of the greatest importance because, through it, the individual can find himself in the Most High and triumph over all fear.

The triumph of fear is always proof that the individual is dispossessed of his being. It is the signature of the enemies of humanity. Do not allow yourself to be enslaved by fear; instead, find within yourself the force which can always lead you higher, in the great protection of God and of his omnipresent love.

Mastering The Fire Of Love

In order to find true peace, one must possess the fire. Only the fire of love gives one the strength to face everything, to conquer everything, to undertake everything. The person who is in love is capable of anything in order to rejoin his beloved. The fire of love consumes all of the fences, all of the barriers and boundaries, all of the insults and taboos. The person who is truly in love is valiant, courageous, determined, inspired, wise, ardent, and ready to rush towards the fortress of the spirit in order to earn the price of his love. Why do human beings let the fire of love, the fire of life, go out?

To be alive, one must be in love. But not just with a person or a limited idea, because a limited love always ends. One must be in love with the limitless, with the infinite; and that is when the fire can take on its whole dimension.

The discovery of fire revolutionized the history of humanity. In the beginning, fire served life; and now it serves death and destruction. Why haven't human beings seen the obvious? Because they have not gone any farther than the physical plane, and have ignored the point of view of life, of feelings, of thoughts, of the soul, of the spirit. The fire of love must rise all the way up to the limitless spirit, by passing through one's life, one's feelings, one's thoughts and one's soul.

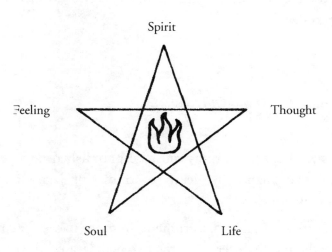

Only by raising themselves all the way up to the spirit can human beings build peace. Only in the spirit can unity be found and achieved. From this unity comes the perfect harmony which can then become a reality in our actions.

Humanity has lost control of the fire of love. Human beings cannot be in love when they want to be, and do not know how to direct their fire towards the Sublime One, towards the Most High. So, they lose their life, their feelings, their thoughts, their souls and their spirits. They are totally incapable of achieving peace; their pentagram is inverted.

How much time will human beings need in order to understand that the person whose pentagram is inverted cannot achieve true peace, and that this is why the whole world has failed to do so—in spite of all of its attempts? It just gets worse and worse.

Christ wants to bring us a fire—that is, a new love which heals and elevates higher; in contrast, the old love is a source of conflicts, of tears and of gnashing of teeth. This fire disturbs those who want to sleep.

Handling The Sword Of Decisions

The sword that he brings must be brandished and used. This means that man must learn to think for himself—which is absolutely not easy.

He must develop discernment, in order to see for himself the two paths and their servants, the two pentagrams, the two kinds of peace, the two humanities. Then he must make his choice—make a free and conscious decision. The sword also allows him to show initiative, to become a creator for peace.

This sword must not be turned towards another person or towards the outside, but towards oneself, because man's true enemies are always living inside of him. The war that Christ came to bring is a victory over oneself—a mastery, a conquest of oneself. This involves a spontaneous internal revolt, and the apparition of the spirit of awakening.

Through his words, Christ showed that only his teaching, clearly understood, can bring peace, because it is based upon a perfect knowledge of the constitution of man and of the universe. No peace can last if there is no harmonization of the part with the Whole.

Others are satisfied just to wish for peace and to debate over it in lofty television programs; but it goes no further than that—it's completely ineffective. It's even a miracle if they don't end up insulting each other during the discussion. But how could someone who has neither found nor achieved peace inside himself create it on the outside? This is obviously a case of the blind leading the blind. It is absolutely not necessary to be clairvoyant to know that peace will never be established as a result of such debates. They're always talking about eliminating something in the world, or about creating something else which would supposedly produce peace. But peace cannot be artificial; it must draw its foundation from the depths. The flower's perfume fills the air because the flower is a flower. An artificial flower has no perfume. The kingdom of peace is like a flower's perfume—filling the atmosphere with its fragrance. External peace flows naturally from the inner peace that is profoundly experienced. Therefore, we must not allow others—some elite group—to decide in our place what kind of peace we are going to live with. Individual and universal peace is everyone's business.

The Negative Being Makes Everything Harmful; The Positive Being Makes Everything Beneficial

In these televised debates, we also notice that each person defends his own opinion above all, and accuses the others—his adversaries on the subject of peace—of being instigators of war. Each one plants himself firmly upon his own positions.

Everyone wants peace, and war is breaking out all over the place. The intention is good; it's the method and the knowledge of peace that are erroneous.

There is not one single country on the planet that is not at war. Confrontations, violence and conflicts exist in every country, even if we don't see the soldiers and we don't hear the devastating sound of the weapons.

The majority of human beings are at war with themselves, with other people, and with the universe.

Peace is a higher state of consciousness and of life which very few people have come to know. It is a sacred order where everything is in its proper place, and where harmony and purity reign.

What human beings call "peace" is, in reality, a lull in the storm, a period of tranquility which allows them to go about their petty business—which, precisely, leads to war. This peace is a kind of death—a peace of the tomb, where there is nothing happening anymore. Everyone feels that creative activity is preferable to this kind of passive peace—because at least we feel alive, awake and conscious. The person who is going into a fight wakes up; he is vigilant, conscious, self-possessed, determined. So war has an awakening side. But, in the fight, in the work for peace, there is no negative suffering; everything becomes just and good, everything is inspired by love and the highest wisdom.

The artisan of peace can say: *"My Father-Mother works, and I, too, work; I am one with Him."* Peace is not death; on the contrary, it generates life and an overabundance of activity—for a goal that is sublime, celestial, divine and magnificent.

Human beings, in their ignorance of the two kinds of peace, think that, if war, sickness and everything negative would just disappear forever, then they would be in living in happiness and peace; they do not realize that they themselves are the source of war and negativity, and that this is a means for awakening and acquiring wisdom. Without negativity, human beings would be dead. There is nothing negative about war in itself; but, if a being is negative, then he makes everything harmful—whereas, if he is positive, he leads everything into the light. Therefore, war, as a virtue, can become something very positive, very stimulating—with the spirit of conquest, of respect for life, and of the aspiration to elevate oneself, to become perfect. Peace can become negative through stagnation, the rejection of the evolution which is God's will for creation, laziness and apathy. War and peace are two complementary virtues which must mutually balance and stimulate each other. Everything that the cosmic intelligence has created is good and just. It is human beings who, in turning away from the celestial order to do everything their own way, generate evil by using the forces placed at their disposal in an inappropriate way. This is when a war and a negative peace appear. The only way to make them disappear is to look for the real fight and for the holy peace. We must give war and peace a new orientation—more spiritual, nobler, more internalized—and bring about a fundamental reversal within ourselves.

The Work Of The Masters

Know that the external world is a mirror of your internal world and of your self. You see in the world only what you carry inside yourself. The person who is filled with hatred, dissatisfaction and injustice looks at the world through the eyes of vengeance. The person who is in love with life looks at things through the eyes of love, of beauty and of poetry.

Thus, the world is the way that you look at it; and it reflects your own image.

One must strive to see the world through the eyes of love, wisdom and truth. It is this kind of vision that leads to peace.

Let human beings understand these sacred laws of the spirit, and realize that what they carry inside themselves is the most important thing. Passive, dead peace is a dead-end. Only the person who has achieved celestial peace inside himself, through his own efforts, can project it and find it outside himself. If you want to see peace on the outside, you will have to already possess a fragment, a parcel, of it inside yourself. It has always been the role of the artisans of peace to transmit seeds of peace, through the Schools of mysteries spread all over the earth, in order to open up the internal eyes of their students. This sacred transmission takes place in silence and in an etheric way. In the ancient tradition of the light, this stage was called "Entering the Aura of a Master". "Master" is the title given to a man or a woman who has achieved the holy peace internally, and who has, therefore, become a member and a servant of the hierarchy of the cosmic order. Externally, this Master is similar to all other human beings, but entering his aura means coming to know his secret inner life and receiving a seed of true peace. The person who does not receive this seed has no criterion for distinguishing between true and false peace. This is why Christ says that he has come to sow war and division in the world, and not to lull human beings to sleep—but, instead, to awaken them to life and to the I-Am-individuality. The person who wants to numb your consciousness is hoping to put you into chains and to dominate you. Only the person who gives you the keys to free inner awakening wants to lead you into the true light.

The Five Stages On The Path Of Peace

The seed of division which Christ aspires to sow is that of discernment, of criterion. The individual who receives the seed of peace perceives that, in the world, there exists a conspiracy of silence, a bewitchment, a collective hypnosis, which keeps human beings on the wrong path—the path of suffering. Then he understands the meaning of the royal fight, of work, and of fundamental reversal.

In his words, Christ starts with division—that is, by introducing a new image of peace, he reveals the false peace. Truth uncovers lies and reality unmasks illusion. This division generates the virtue of discernment, which is the beginning of all healthy development. Without discernment, the individual swallows everything that people want to make him swallow—without comparing, without thinking. But, in order to possess this critical spirit, it is necessary to know the two points of view, to have no prejudices oneself.

After discernment, Christ brings fire, because the disciple must develop inside himself the love for the new idea of peace. It is love that gives strength and accomplishes the preparatory work. From love is born the aspiration towards the new vision of peace.

Without the fire of love, no transformation is possible inside the disciple, and the seed falls onto infertile ground.

The stage of the sword appears all by itself when the fire has reached maturity. The disciple has merged internally with the idea of the new peace; he has achieved stability. And now, in order to go farther, he has to make a decision; he has to use the sword to sever his remaining ties with the egregor of false peace, of the false teaching which leads to the kingdom of death.

This sword is the symbol of an internal force which lives inside of every person in this world—the force of the "I-ray". When the disciple has found his true being, all he has to do is to manifest it by means of the sword.

This is when the stage of war appears, but it is not a war as conceived by the world; instead, it is more like a healing, a transmutation of the negative into positive, a pacification, and, especially, a sacred endeavor in cosmic harmony for the triumph of Supreme Good, of the light without shadows.

You can see that there really is an entire science contained in these simple words of Christ; and only the person who has lived them on the inside can understand them, because these are eternal truths which belong to all beings.

Through these words "about peace", Christ describes, in a veiled manner, the stages on the path of peace:

First – disillusionment: *I have not come to bring the false peace of the world, inside which human beings can carry on their petty scheming without being disturbed. This peace leads to destruction, or to reformation through suffering.*

Second – awakening and discernment: *I, the I-Am, the true being of all beings—I have come to separate the good seed from the bad, the truth from the lie, eternity from time, and life from death, so that each person will be able to understand who he is in truth, and will no longer take the ephemeral shadows of the world for eternal realities.*

Third – the elevation of the inner being: *Having recognized who you are in truth—through discernment and through the separation of the infinite from the finite, of the eternal from the transitory, of your true being from your mortal self—understand that the self can be elevated and ennobled if it aspires to the light with its whole being. For this, it is necessary to nourish an inner fire for the noble, the good, the true.*

Fourth – the integral transformation of the inner being: *Having merged "on high" with the true being that you are eternally, now learn how to handle its creative force in order to achieve inside yourself, in the reality of the earth and through your actions, the peace which does not come from this world.*

Fifth – the incorporation into the cosmic hierarchy: *Your Heavenly Father-Mother works, and you work, too—one with Him in the accomplishment of His will.*

As one who aspires to serve peace, you must pass through these five stages:

1) Begin by thinking for yourself, and by looking at the world, in its globality, through new eyes. Notice that the paths of the world all lead to a dead-end—death. Look for a new path which leads to the life that is constantly renewed—the inner path.

2) Strive to awaken within the "here and now". Look for what is always the same inside of you, what does not change, the source of your being; and find, also, what changes and is transformed.

Find what is most important in life by meditating on this idea: "What will be left of me in one trillion years?"

This meditation must absolutely not make you feel discouraged, but, instead, bring you more strength, more joie de vivre, more energy, etc.

3) Be in love with the universal teaching; love the celestial order, the cosmic harmony. If you are not in love with the eternal wisdom, you cannot receive the teaching in the right way. Only the pure fire of true love allows the disciple to be on the right wavelength and to progress along the path. Learn to set yourself on fire for the high ideas of the divine teaching. Consider that, behind theses ideas, there are highly evolved beings, and send them all of your love. Do this consciously, because "practice makes perfect".

Through this method of setting yourself on fire for the universal teaching, you will project forces towards the spiritual world which will nourish your soul and open up to you the kingdom of the free spirit.

This is a very powerful method for gaining access to the higher worlds, because fire is an invisible magic door.

4) Learn to find the strength that is inside of you and to make use of it for what is good. Find the impulse of your true I and, behind it, that of the great I-Am; and learn to make decisions and to make your actions originate from this impulse. Be aware that your I-ray is your sword of light, the force which allows you to undertake everything and to succeed at everything.

From the moment when you take possession of this sword, you become a true initiate.

Learn to govern your life from your true I, and not under the multiple influences of the personality and of the conditions of the outside world.

5) Look for ways in which you could, on your level, participate in the healthy and harmonious evolution of the earth and of humanity.

Do not feel like an isolated and irresponsible being any longer, but like a cell of the cosmos and a free being who is responsible for his actions.

Seek to unite yourself, in liberty, with other beings who aspire to work on the same ray as you. The person who seeks peace just for himself alone is not an artisan of peace. The peace created within the community of the servants of good is the promise of a new heaven and of a new earth for all of humanity. It is an immutable law that what is created within the bosom of the community of light is then radiated out over all the earth and towards all beings.

The servants of the light fight with the weapons of the light.

The person who loves his enemy—this is the servant of peace.

The Healing Of The Being Of War

One of the great keys for peace resides in the understanding of this law: "The world is the way that you look at it, because it reflects your own image." Therefore, you cannot place the responsibility for what happens to you in your personal life on anyone else but yourself. Success or failure resides solely within yourself and depends on your correct union with the source of the spirit.

First of all, human beings refuse to look at reality—and, therefore, to be disillusioned. They carry inside themselves the dreams that they want to realize at any cost, without worrying about whether or not they conform to a healthy and harmonious evolution.

Secondly, refusing to look at themselves and to discover their inner world, they prefer to throw the responsibility for a failed and chaotic life onto other people—and, in this way, to enter into conflicts. It's so much easier—never being responsible for anything; one is innocent and perfect—embodying the summit of evolution. Being at the top, one no longer has any need to progress, to transform oneself, to work on oneself; and stagnation appears—the source of all wars.

The person who turns the sword against himself and who triumphs as Christ teaches him to—this person courageously faces his own inner conflict; and, as a result, the source of all outside aggression is stopped.

This is the key.

The man who has triumphed over himself no longer takes his own internal conflict out on others. He has turned his pentagram around, and he has found serenity; he has reversed his polarity—he becomes positive.

Thus, in the present state of the world, it is impossible not to make war, because it is inscribed inside evolution. What is possible is to transform this energy of war into a positive, beneficial, salutary force.

What? What was that? What is he telling us here? War turned into something beneficial? He must be delirious! He's become a little too illuminated!

It is precisely because all of the pacifists systematically reject war that they fail in their attempts at peace. If war exists on the earth, it is because it has a purpose to serve inside evolution. Peace can never be built upon the fear and the exclusion of one element of creation.

All beings must be invited to participate in peace—or else, peace is not possible; it is a false peace, guided by hidden interests.

Peace is universal; it includes all of the beings, visible and invisible, in creation, within a mutual respect and a common endeavor—or it is not.

War and everything negative must not be excluded from evolution, but must take an active part. In this way, everything becomes just and good.

Therefore, every person must go to war with himself—conquer himself, surpass himself, and know himself in what is the most beautiful and the most noble. The Master St. John points out this internal battle against oneself in his Apocalypse when he says: *"To the one who will conquer, I will give..."* This idea of Triumph implies an idea of combat; this is the initiatic quest of the being who aspires to the supreme light. If human beings do not understand the meaning of this initiatic quest for oneself, then peace is not possible. Here, it is necessary to underline the fact that the consumer society does nothing in this direction, and that everything goes in the opposite direction.

To Be Or Not To Be—That Is The Question

Human beings must finally grow up and understand that the many battles against other people, against the world, and against ideals are, in reality, nothing more than a ruse—to run away from oneself and to avoid the transformation required by evolution.

Facing peace and evolution, man must question himself. There is no other way.

But, faced with this evidence of evolution, man understands that he is called to transform himself; and this gives rise inside of him to the idea that, deep down, he is not—but that he is constantly becoming. He is not because he does not really know himself, but lives on the surface of his being. Thus, he is afraid of disappearing in death, afraid of what he might find if he awakens his inner life. This is a feeling that is buried very deep in the human soul, and it produces, inside every individual, an uneasiness that was marvelously interpreted by Shakespeare:

"To be or not to be—that is the question."

Yes, that is the big question that one must ask oneself very forcefully. Peace is dependent upon it.

For example, the fact that most human beings do not like solitude and silence comes from their innate fear of being alone with themselves and of seeing their inner life appear—along with its many questions. Silence is filled with words and interrogations. Christ speaks of solitude as a state to be attained. When all is said and done, this is about living inside oneself and finding oneself, which necessitates traveling down a long road filled with traps—which only a warrior or a knight can negotiate successfully. Along this road, dragons are going to rise up.

The Accumulation Of Discontentment—The Source Of War

When a man is ready to fight, it's because he is under pressure. But he does not see that the source of this pressure resides, above all, inside himself. It is an accumulation of discontentment. Some people unload this discontentment onto their entourage on a regular basis; others keep it to themselves, accumulating it inside until the day when the barricades give way and everything explodes.

There are several techniques which teach you how to get rid of your aggressiveness and your internal sickness, how to channel it. But, in reality, this doesn't help at all, because the question remains suspended in mid-air: *"To be or not to be."*

The interest of war and of all conflicts is to unload our violence and our anger onto someone else—making that other person responsible for us, for our own non-existence, for our spiritual laziness. Human beings continue to crucify Christ every day and, deep down, they are ashamed; they are not proud of themselves, and feel the need to release the pressure that they accumulate in this way.

The peace that they advocate is one of cowardliness and running away.

The person who agrees to take a long, hard look at himself, who wants to know who he is in truth, in the heights of the spirit, who unites himself with his inner Christ, his own Christ-like consciousness, no longer has any inner conflict. The source of discontentment is dried up, and he no longer feels any need to fight with other people. Instead, he wants to build the kingdom of peace and harmony that he is experiencing inside himself. What comes out of him is positive, because he himself is positive—now that he is united with the source of all life, wisdom and love. His pentagram is turned around, and there is no longer any conflict inside of him; he is one with himself and with the Whole.

The Image And The Influence Of The Devil

The person who is in harmony with God, with the source of the being and of existence, is at peace, and becomes an artisan of peace.

The person who is not in harmony with God—that is, with his own higher consciousness—is at war, and becomes a carrier, an agent, of war and negativity in the world.

This is an infallible criterion; but it just so happens that the trap, the obstacle, comes from the fact that human beings do not want to recognize that they are agents of war—that their inverted pentagrams produce the image of the goat, of evil. They do not want to face this image inside themselves, which the Rose+Cross calls the guardian of the threshold—the accumulation of the negative karma of oneself and of humanity. They prefer to think that they are good, wonderful, authentic, divine beings. They choose to delude themselves, to lie to themselves. It's fabulous how we can always find good reasons for performing the most monstrous of actions. Pictures showing Hitler with his family were censored for dozens of years because a certain intelligentsia was afraid of shocking the world by showing the Fuhrer playing with children, smiling, full of love for his wife, in the intimacy of his home, away from all propaganda. Yes, Hitler was an ordinary man, with a man's feelings; but that did not stop him from ordering monstrous and criminal acts—surely, with a clear conscience and a self-justification. Human beings said that Hitler was the devil, the incarnation of evil. But the truth is that the devil does not exist, and that it is human beings who bring him to life. If they hadn't voted for Hitler, he would have had no power at all; he would not even have existed. Every unconscious man—giving up his intelligence to the instinctive force, walking with his head down, refusing to cultivate his inner life—forms the image of the inverted pentagram, in which the head of the devil appears—that is, the mean and vengeful God, who punishes those who violate the law of universal love. All of those people who vote unconsciously for people like Hitler generate all of the wars and atrocities in the world.

In his I-Am ray, the individual is free to conquer his being and to serve the celestial order, the cosmic harmony—or to give up his being and put himself at the service of the great just-anything. He calls upon the devil—that is, misfortune, mass destruction, and reformation through suffering.

Today, almost all human beings put themselves at the service of the great just-anything, while giving themselves airs of holiness, of benefactors of humanity, etc. And the worst part is that they get sucked into the game and believe all of their lies.

The beginning of peace is looking at oneself just as one is and not being afraid of facing the negative image that will appear. No matter how black that image is, it can be turned around and transformed. The inverted pentagram of black magic can become the flaming star that guides the wise men towards the place of Christ's birth.

The three wise men represent the triple personality—with the thoughts, the feelings and the actions. The birth of Christ reveals a light which is found behind these three faculties of the personality, and which the correctly prepared disciple can discover.

These are great initiatic secrets concerning the correct education of the human being.

Then, the diabolical image is transformed into light, and peace becomes possible.

The words "God" and "Devil" have the same root, to indicate that they draw their origin from the same source. God represents the positive side, and the Devil the negative side, of a single and unique reality. The positive can very well become negative, and vice versa—the devil can become divine, celestial, beneficent. It is the individual that is at the center of these two energies.

Peace Resides Beyond The Illusory Appearances

So human beings do not have to be afraid of finding something negative inside themselves, because this is completely normal at our stage of evolution and we must accept it—not in order to stagnate, but to work on ourselves and become positive. The person who discharges the negativity that he carries inside himself onto another person becomes a true artisan of destruction in the world. He says to himself: "Why should I make the effort to work on myself in order to become good? All I have to do is say, imagine and proclaim that I am good, and discharge all of the bad onto other people." Since no man can live with a bad self-image, there exists this kind of false therapy of creating a good one artificially for oneself. This is a kind of make-up—and we are living in the age of the facelift and of all kinds of cosmetic surgery. Christ used the term "whitened sepulcher". Everything is beautiful and resplendent on the outside—but, inside, behind the facade, everything is rotten, in a state of decomposition.

Human beings spend more and more time working on their bodies and their appearance; one must take care of one's image. But which is the most important: the image that we give of ourselves, or the one that we truly are—the one that visits us in the silence when we are alone? Where is the soul's place in all of this?

By only taking care of what is superficial, we finish up by losing what is essential—and by being uprooted and cut off from the source.

Because human beings don't know who they are in truth, they have invented a whole cast of characters, of roles, which they play out marvelously in life. Often it is life itself, and its external circumstances, which design the role; and the individual finishes by getting caught up in the game. It's these illusions that help us to live, that push us forward and encourage us—and, in that way, they are beneficial; but peace necessitates being conscious and finding the true being.

Illusions and pretty pictures are for children; but the child must grow up and understand the meaning of life. To be a human being is, precisely, to be an artisan of peace; it is, very simply, being oneself in the light—being true. From this kind of inner stability inside the truth come peace, harmony, equilibrium and beauty.

Becoming an adult, a true human being, is not easy; it is a high ideal which requires a long apprenticeship. If you think that being a human being is easy, then you are already on the path of illusion.

To be a human being, it is not enough just to have the form of one. The form is just a garment; it is the spirit that vivifies.

Today we are in the age of the instantaneous—of automatic dispensers, of the no-effort-required, etc. They want to make us believe that all we have to do is push a button in order to get everything that we desire. But what sensible and spiritual being can believe in peace in pill-form, in dehydrated peace, in peace with no effort required of oneself? This is the peace of zombies, of the living dead, of cemeteries, of the abdication of humanity—the peace of the sleeping pills and the ostriches, the peace of the cowards who give up their souls because it's easier that way. The easy path is the wrong path. Life is full of trials, which we must overcome—because it is the obstacle that reveals to us who we are.

The Paths Of The Two Kinds Of Peace

The person who wants to avoid the tests only proves that he has not prepared himself well enough for life. He is still a child inside. For the person who is correctly prepared, tests are not negative; they allow maturity to appear. The more you run away from the tests, the more you weaken yourself; you cross over into illusion, into a false image of yourself—and you feel kind of sick inside. The more you face the tests, the more hardened you become—and the more you grow up, and awaken, and become what you are.

Solar initiation has always had only one, single goal: to turn a human being in form into a human being in spirit—a man of light, his own master, servant of Good, artisan of peace.

Counter-initiation aspires to create artificial human beings, genetically manipulated clones—without a soul, without a consciousness, without their own will, melted into the masses without a trace of originality.

This is what is at stake—clearly exposed—and it is up to each person to choose his side, and his future.

On one side, a so-called easy path—but which is, in reality, the most twisting and terrifying. The lie appears easier at first; but, in the long run, it is much more complicated. This is an endless spiral, inside which one loses everything.

On the other side, a more difficult path, which requires effort, working on oneself, and an awakening of the consciousness, the heart and the soul—but which, in the long run, is easier, because love gives you wings.

The Technique Of Harmony And Of Cosmic Unification

It is impossible to find one's humanity in a surprise package; this is something of value, which must be deserved, and obtained through one's own work and ability.

If we think and teach openly that to be a human being is to do just anything and to live just any way, then we can be sure that peace will never be achieved. Without peace, there is no true life, no consciousness, no joy, no happiness, no success.

To be a human being is to make one's life conform to a celestial, cosmic order.

The technique is simple in its outline.

First, you develop the habit of entering into silence and of producing a state of calm inside your soul. Then, you open yourself up to the living nature and you observe it until you feel inside yourself an infinite impression of harmony, of celestial order. Everything is in a magical, divine order. You can also get this feeling by contemplating the starlit sky or by cultivating certain thoughts.

This feeling of an unchangeable order—and of a cosmic intelligence standing behind it—is the first step towards finding peace and becoming an authentic human being.

The second step consists of looking inside oneself to find this perfect order once again. You may find it when you look at your physical body; but, when you take a look inside your personality, your thoughts, your feelings and your actions, it's disorder and anarchy that you are going to discover. All of that is not in perfect harmony with the cosmos, with the Whole. Deep inside you, there are seeds of war, of anarchy, of conflict, and of disorder. The least little thought that does not conform is enough to destroy the atmosphere of peace.

The cosmic order is based on a law of love and harmony. As soon as you break this law, you are in conflict with the cosmos, and with your deeper being—which is one with the Whole. Thus, you create an inner conflict which divides you and turns you into an agent of war.

All you have to do, for example, is borrow some money from a friend and not give it back to him—and you can lose your peace, your health, your life; or you might fall madly in love with your neighbor's wife, etc. Peace is a sacred science, a mastery, an illumination of the spirit. When a division is created inside someone, the war starts raging—and the individual unconsciously feels a chaotic energy gnawing away at him from the inside. He is nervous, irritable, tense. Only the person who is one with himself and with the cosmos knows peace.

The person who pays attention to himself perceives that the battle is internal and that it emanates from a violation of the law of universal love, and from the breaking of the bond which united him to his true being. He is no longer in accord with himself, with the cosmos, and with the Supreme Being—the source of life.

An out-of-tune instrument can only produce discordant sounds—even in the middle of the best orchestra, and even in the hands of the most talented musician. The first thing to do is to tune it. This is when an internal struggle begins; the instrument must be put back into harmony with the Whole once again. The war energy becomes positive again; the sword is turned against oneself. It is because of this conscious inner conflict—designed to re-establish the celestial order inside oneself—that unity can be found. The disciple begins by separating what is positive from what is negative; he strives to know himself in his higher nature and in his lower nature. Then he desires to commune more and more with the Supreme One—and to muzzle his lower nature. This can go on for a while—until the day when he perceives that a new center of perception has appeared inside of him. He can see the higher and the lower natures simultaneously—without identifying with them; he has become the one who observes—the summit of the triangle, which unites the two opposing sides.

He is the source of the positive as well as the negative, and he is the one who decides what he must do. A new being appears inside of him—Christ, the true man; the artisan of peace comes to take the reins and to unify everything inside the light.

The Peace That The World Does Not Know

From the internal war comes the true peace, the celestial peace, the cosmic order, unification—the peace that the world does not know.

This true peace has been, throughout all time, the privilege and the science of the initiates. Those who talk about peace without having committed themselves to this path of self-transformation and spiritual rebirth are liars and storytellers who delude themselves in order to better deceive others. Their intention to build peace is beneficent, but intention is not enough. Peace does not have to be built in the world because it is already there. The whole cosmos sings the song of peace, and all we have to do is open ourselves up to it with our childlike souls, and then make our inner life conform to the celestial order and the cosmic teaching. This is so simple that even a child could do it; but it requires colossal efforts, which only the humble and gentle-hearted are capable of accomplishing.

The Person Who Wants To Keep His Illusions Is Not Ready For Peace

Why is it that human beings no longer go and ask the advice of the initiates—of those who have achieved mastery? Quite simply, because they have understood that, if they wanted to keep their illusions, they would be knocking on the wrong door. They want peace without making any effort, without transforming and questioning themselves. The peace that they want to build is a calamity, an oppression of minorities, a form of tyranny in the name of good, and a disguised violation of human rights, of the hierarchy and of the creator.

When the rich young man comes to the Master Jesus in order to obtain the kingdom of God—that is, the treasure of light, for which peace is the door—he expects Christ to serve it up to him on a silver platter, by means of some magic trick. But there are no magic tricks in nature.

The Master advises him to follow the ten commandments—that is, to follow a discipline in his external life. The young man answers that he already follows that discipline—so the Master then opens up the door for him: *"Sell all that you have, give it to the poor, and follow me."* This is not advice to be taken literally, but, instead, a technique for the inner life. It is easy to abandon what one has on the outside, but much more difficult to perform this same operation deep inside oneself. It is necessary to accept the undeniable fact that human beings cannot achieve peace in their present state. First they have to change their internal state. The only way to give them the peace that they desire is to kill them or to dope them up with medication—or any of the other ways so widely used in our day. In our present-day culture, we find it much easier to dope ourselves up than to awaken. This is a fact!

Almost everything is designed to put the human consciousness to sleep—to limit it, to imprison it, and to control it.

When the individual finds peace in his present state of development, it means that he is moving towards death—that his internal fight has stopped—without having achieved illumination. The man accepts his situation; he signs a compromise, a passive collaboration—he abdicates.

Sometimes we hear that a person has found peace at the end of his life, but this is not the same thing at all. He has destroyed everything, and spent all of his energy on worthless things, and now he has nothing left—so he gives up and just lets himself go under; but that is not peace.

Peace Is Not A Box Of Sleeping Pills

How can one be at peace in a world like ours? Is the heart at peace? Yes, the heart is at peace—but it's a different peace. The one which consists of accomplishing one's duty—of not living only selfishly, but of working for the good of all beings. The heart is at peace because it is pure; it is truly itself. But, if approach your heart filled with love, it will give you not peace but work; and if you accomplish it, then you will approach peace. If you do not do your duty, you distance yourself from the heart and from peace.

We must stop telling ourselves all kinds of ridiculous stories.

These days, we think that we are going to find peace and happiness, and succeed in life, without having a light to guide us, without working, without an ideal—by living only for ourselves in complete tranquility.

The teaching of peace is not a varnish or a coat of paint used to hide the fact that the wood is rotten. The person who finds peace in an external way becomes mummified, because he wants to escape from the transformation required by the law of evolution.

So peace is not a comfort—even a spiritual one. Sometimes comfort is necessary, because we need to rest to get our strength back; but this is always so that we can get going again with even more energy. The person who longs for permanent comfort is immature. Often comfort is a protective illusion which prevents the initiatic spark. The person who longs to keep his illusions is not yet ready for peace.

There is no true peace inside illusion.

The person who is using initiatic teaching to look for a higher authority capable of justifying him in his illusions is making a mistake; he is knocking at the wrong door. Those who sell dreams and miracles are the ones who want to put you to sleep in order to steal your treasure of light. The false priests of all religions, along with politicians, are the champions in this domain.

God Has No Side: He Is Indivisible

When a being like Christ or Buddha appears in the world, he leaves no one indifferent. Some are on his side, others against him; this is inevitable. Thus, the greatest good, the greatest blessing—the incarnation of a son of God on earth—becomes a source of division, of conflict, of war. Those who are for Christ are the positive ones and the others are the negative ones; but, in fact, neither group has more value than the other. Being for Christ without entering into his teaching and becoming Christ oneself is just one more foolish dream. We want to have a clear conscience, to justify ourselves by putting ourselves on the side of good—of God. But God has no side; he is one, indivisible. He is everything—uniting everything.

All those who want to make themselves at home on the earth and establish themselves in the world must pay the price of blood, the baptism of the world. Thus, the Catholic Church has spilled blood in the name of Christ. It has not deviated from the rule; it has signed the mysterious pact. Only the Church or the School of St. John has not spilled any blood; it has always remained pure and faithful. It has committed itself to the true path of light, and has chosen not to be of the world.

The whole world knows about the Master Jesus, and his coming is something that transformed humanity. That's a fact. He brought something divine, sublime, magnificent and pure into the world. Those who are afraid of the divine have insulted and discredited him in many ways, both quietly and overtly. Those who aspire to a life that is nobler, more beautiful and more rewarding, those who feel their sleeping souls deep inside of them, have marvelled at this being who embodied their secret ideal and their hope. But the fact is that it is not enough just to place this being on a pedestal and fall asleep in his shadow. His image, placed outside oneself, must create a deep conflict. On the one side, there is Jesus, the Master, the prototype for the humanity of light; and, on the other side, there is me. If I want to resolve the conflict, I must become one with him; and, for that, I, too—like him—must find the true being that I am eternally and unite myself with the Heavenly Father-Mother. This is what the Master St. John was the first to accomplish. He became Christ and opened up the path to all human beings. The true path—of peace, of brotherhood-sisterhood, of happiness, and of success.

Through his words, Christ has given us all of the keys to achieve the peace of the kingdom of light. These words are not easy to understand; we must meditate upon them over and over again.

> "Human beings may think that I have come to bring peace into the world; they do not know that I have come to sow division on the earth—fire, the sword, war. Because, where there are five in one house, three will be against two and two against three—the father against the son, the son against the father; they will all stand alone."

THE KINGDOM OF PEACE IS LIKE A VILLAGE

The kingdom of peace is like a village situated at the foot of a high mountain. In beautiful weather, the inhabitants can contemplate its snow-covered summit cut out against the deep-blue sky. Most of the villagers are happy just with this view, knowing the dangers of the mountain; but the more audacious ones set out on the great adventure of conquering the summit. Having reached it, they discover a new viewpoint, a new life—a new ascension of an internal, invisible mountain.

The person who aspires to always raise himself up higher cannot do anything else but begin the climb up to the heavens—once he has reached the highest mountaintops in the world.

In truth, I say to you: peace is a summit. It is always the end-result of hard work requiring a lot of effort, of a whole path sprinkled with hopes, idealism and struggles. Those who stay down in the valley and are satisfied with the view off in the distance are depending on the external circumstances of life, because, at any moment, the clouds can hide the summit of peace from them. By staying where they are, they cannot evolve.

The climbing of the summit of peace belongs to the living, to the courageous, to the strong-willed idealists. When the summit is reached, the will stops, and peace settles in and is experienced deep inside; a new life begins, a new horizon appears, a new solar kingdom spreads out as far as the eye can see.

Achieving peace results in the perception of a kingdom which remains invisible to those who are afraid and satisfied with their tiny lives.

The person whose lungs do not long to inhale the universe will run out of breath on the high summits of the pure spirit, where the air of the every-man-for-himself becomes very thin.

THE GREAT MEDITATION: THE TREE OF PEACE

The Double-Edged Sword of the Archangel Michael

Christ says: *"I have not come to bring peace, but the sword."*

The sword of the Archangel Michael produces self-knowledge. It cuts and separates, and lets the true light appear beyond the fog of illusion.

The person who is not touched by this sword cannot approach the holy and true peace. This is the deep and secret meaning of the act of dubbing in knighthood. It is when he is touched by the sword that the candidate becomes a knight; he enters the aura of the Archangel Michael, and he commits himself to becoming a servant, a defender, a soldier of peace.

Modern man has no great spiritual cause to defend because he is mixed-up—he doesn't know who he is anymore; he no longer knows how to discern the elements which make up his composition. He is incapable of saying which things inside of him come from the spirit, the soul or the body.

If he is hungry, he doesn't know who is hungry; is it him, his consciousness, his spirit or his body? The body is hungry and it is the consciousness which points this out to him; but the consciousness doesn't get hungry—nor does the spirit.

The body is dependent on the earth and on its cosmic environment.

The consciousness is dependent on the body—on its purity and its composition.

The spirit is a pure, eternal, unchangeable flame which draws its origin from the divinity.

If you want to become a real artisan of peace, cultivate the virtue of discernment; learn to separate the things inside of you, so that you will be able to compare them better and to become more aware of them.

Clearly discern your body, your consciousness, and your spirit; and understand their respective laws.

Your body comes from matter. It needs the living nature in order to stay alive and develop. Without the earth's magnetism—and without food, water, air, the sun, colors, etc.—it cannot keep itself alive.

The relationship between the body and the living nature generates the personal self—with its desires, its feelings, and its thoughts.

The consciousness is like a mirror, or like the surface of a lake. It can reflect the sky of the spirit, but, for that, its water must be calm—and that depends on the body and the personal self. If the body and the personal self are not in harmony, then the consciousness becomes blurred; it loses the vision of the spirit, and life loses its meaning and its stability.

The double-edged sword is the consciousness, which is placed between the body and the spirit. If you want to walk in the light, you must learn to handle the sword of your consciousness.

Exercise of the Internal Awakening of the Consciousness

To begin with, awaken inside yourself by becoming aware of yourself regularly throughout the day.

Next, really try to find some moments of solitude, where everything is calm. In these moments, concentrate on your consciousness—purify it, clarify it, expand it; and, finally, turn it towards the immortal, eternal, infinite spirit, in order to capture celestial impressions. The more you are able to unite your consciousness with the solar flame of your spirit, the more peace, order and harmony will establish themselves in your life.

Strive also to become aware of your body and of its relationship with the living nature. Look at what you eat and how you eat. Pay attention to your breathing and learn to breathe consciously. Be careful of what you drink and how you drink. Analyze your relationship with the light and the sun, and with life in general.

If you perform this exercise correctly, you will perceive very quickly that your consciousness is determined by the way in which you experience all of these things. Either it is weakened, or it is enriched.

If you eat, drink, breathe and live just anything and in just any way—without recognition, without gratitude, without joy, unconsciously—then your consciousness and your life become dark; you plunge yourself into the darkness of the limitation of the spirit, and you attract pain, suffering, and unhappiness to yourself. Peace is impossible for you; you become determined to be unhappy with everything, and to be irritable, quick-tempered, proud, weak, stupid, pretentious, etc.—in short, all of the ingredients for becoming a servant of the negative cause's forces of decomposition.

Since your earthly self is dependent upon your body, your desires, your feelings and your thoughts, it, too, becomes dark, and your consciousness sinks into a state of hypnosis; you don't know who you are anymore, and you seek only to satisfy the ambitions of your body, to the detriment of your consciousness-your own being-and of your divine spirit. If you ask Christ for peace, it will be a peace of the body—a negative, maleficent, illusory peace.

Peace cannot be built upon a lack of equilibrium. Peace appears all by itself when harmony and justice are re-established. When peace is absent, this reveals the presence of a deep illness and anarchy. This is an infallible criterion. If you do not know peace, it simply proves that you must not rest; instead, it is urgent that you awaken and get to work to introduce the celestial order back into your life and your being.

The sword of the I-Am consciousness says to man: "You are not on the earth simply to eat, drink, sleep, accomplish your little schemes, seize and prosper; instead, you must also learn to give, to improve yourself and to make things better, to obtain the higher knowledge of "knowing yourself" beyond the veil of appearances and of death, to serve the Most High and to accomplish good. Only then will your life be rich, full, joyous and eternal."

Introduce the Light of the Spirit Into Everything You Do

This is a great secret for peace: the state of life determines the state of consciousness, but the state of consciousness determines the state of life. Thus, an unconscious life results in a sleeping consciousness—and a sleeping consciousness in an unconscious life. Introduce the light of the spirit into your consciousness, and it will transform and improve your life.

Introduce light into the actions in your life—make them conscious, beautiful, harmonious and positive; and your consciousness will purify itself and will reflect the magnificence of the spirit.

In accordance with this law, everything that does not conform to the holy law of love, which governs the cosmos, and to the law of harmonious evolution must be progressively eliminated from the life of an artisan of peace. This starts with the smallest things, and continues all the way up to the biggest ones. (1)

---

(1) To delve deeper into this very important subject of the holy law, refer to the chapter entitled "The Origin of Suffering: The Lack of Love" in this author's magnificent book entitled "The Opening of the Rose of the Heart", soon available from Telesma-Evida. (Editor's Note.)

It is necessary to introduce positive currents into our thoughts, our feelings and our desires. Then—as calmness, harmony and clarity appear inside the earthly self—the consciousness becomes capable of reflecting the sky of the spirit.

> The body becomes the Temple of the Most High.
>
> The life unites itself to the universal life.
>
> The will reflects the celestial order.
>
> The heart vibrates with the music of love without boundaries.
>
> The thoughts are illuminated with direct knowledge and the cosmic wisdom.
>
> The consciousness penetrates all of the layers of the being and of the universe, and becomes one with the primary source of the worlds.
>
> Peace is created by the power of the spirit.
>
> Only the spirit of God can create peace, because he is peace.
>
> Without the spirit, the body is not at peace;
>
> the life is not at peace;
>
> the will is not at peace;
>
> the heart is not at peace;
>
> the thoughts are not at peace;
>
> the consciousness is not at peace.

Therefore, doesn't it show great stupidity and great ignorance to look for peace where it cannot be?

How can a person who does not have something possibly give it away? Well, we have to say it: this is a very obvious fact—which those human beings who claim to be the most intelligent and the guides of the planet have not been able to understand and apply. This is why there have never been so many wars in the world; it's the great conflict of everyone against everyone else.

What does humanity gain in all this? Tears, misfortune, suffering, and gnashing of teeth—for a few crumbs of limited happiness. It is against this destiny of stupidity, ignorance and death that one must revolt—by taking one's destiny into one's own hands, and by becoming humble, strong, luminous, good, awakened and courageous.

The Spirit Is Perfect And Matter Is Perfectible

Why can't the body, the heart and the consciousness find peace, happiness and fulfillment? Quite simply, because they are separated, broken up; they contain only pieces. Everything that is separated seeks to be united once again; this is the meaning of life. Everything that is separated is in motion, in development, and can only produce pieces—but never fullness. Only fullness is reality; the rest is ephemeral. The body, the heart and the consciousness produce some crumbs of happiness, joy and peace—but never perfection. They themselves lean towards the perfection which resides in the spirit. The spirit lives in fullness; it is fullness because it is not separated.

The spirit is already perfect, as the Father is perfect; and when Christ invited his disciples to become perfect, he was not talking to their spirits, but to all of the outer shells—the body, the life, the will, the heart, the thoughts, the consciousness, the destiny. In this way, he was once again wielding the sword, because he was creating two poles inside of them—the pole of the spirit, which is perfect, and the pole of matter, which is perfectible. To ask for peace inside matter—that is, immobility—is to fight against the sacred law of evolution; it is to fight against the cosmic intelligence and the forces of good at work within creation. All those who fight against the evolution of matter, and against its transformation and its ennoblement, are the enemies of humanity, who have lost the vision of the sovereign spirit, beyond the outer shells and the form.

The spirit, which is perfect, comes down into matter in order to become aware of itself, through limitation and opposition. Thus, the goal of all of this is to become aware of oneself. The consciousness, appearing in the body by contrast, can once again raise itself up towards the spirit—and take the body with it. In this way, it wins its immortality.

So, all of the people on earth are looking for peace, happiness and fulfillment—but make war because they do not know where to find peace anymore; they are no longer familiar with the path of the spirit, which has been hidden by those who are fighting against evolution.

This is why the true artisan of peace must seek to once again open up inside himself the path of harmonious evolution, of unification and of healthy fulfillment for all of the components and outer shells of his being.

The world, the body, the life, the will, the heart, the thoughts, the consciousness and the destiny must not be considered in a static way, but as elements in motion, which are heading towards perfection, and which rotate around the center of the spirit—which is perfect and without evolution.

Whatever you do in life—whether you are thinking, eating, making love, or sleeping—the spirit must always be present, be invited to join in, because it is the king of creation.

The spirit must always be hovering above you like the omnipresent light of your true, eternal and pure being. It alone has the power to make everything right in your life and to lead everything towards the supreme goal.

The Unity Of The Spirit

Without this convergence of all of the limited parts towards the unity of the spirit, peace is not possible inside oneself or outside of oneself.

Only the unity of the spirit produces peace. If you do not place the divine spirit above everything else in your life and if you do not make everything converge towards it, you disrupt the cosmic order inside yourself—the natural order of things—and you produce an imbalance which leads to illness and death.

Only the cosmic order generates peace. Disorder and anarchy are carriers of war and misfortune.

Only the vision and the presence of the sovereign spirit give a direction to life—the direction of evolution. As soon as this direction is found, all of the components of creation start moving towards self-awakening; this is the beginning of peace. For the body and the earthly self, peace resides in the conscious aspiration of ascension towards the spirit.

The person who does not possess this unity of the spirit sees his consciousness dispersing itself over the four corners of the earth and getting lost in the multiplicity of forms and beings. The more the outer shells move away from the spirit, the more they lose their light and their way—becoming negative and sinking down into the kingdom of the absurd and of death. When absurdity triumphs on all sides, it is the sign that human beings have lost their direction in life and are entering the realm of the great just-anything.

The Balance Between The Spiritual Life And The Material Life

These days, human beings are concerned only with their bodies and with external life. The spirit has disappeared and the consciousness is of no interest to anyone. This orientation produces an imbalance, an unconscious turmoil which is the cause of all wars. Peace is, above all, an equilibrium, a harmony, a fullness, a justice. Man can find this peace only by once again balancing the spirit and matter inside himself—by using the sword of the consciousness.

The sword of the Archangel Michael, which Christ talks about, is the needle on the scale; it is also the virtue which allows one to distinguish what belongs to the spirit from what belongs to matter. Then each thing can be put into its correct place for the good of the whole. One must not neglect the spirit in order to only take care of the material side; but one must not neglect the body either, and take interest only in the spirit. Peace is never extremist; it results from a reasonable union of the two poles of the one-energy.

The Universal Key Of Peace: The Great Method

If you want to approach a deeper understanding of this teaching on peace, you can freely practice the following meditative exercises and methods which emanate from the initiatic current of the Cosmic Tradition and from St. John's humanity of light.

Develop the good habit of feeling the ground under your feet, of feeling that the earth is carrying you. Even when you lie down in your bed to sleep, you can be aware that the earth is supporting you and that you give your body over to it with confidence.

Develop the good habit of feeling the infinite sky above you. You must acquire this perception of the immensity and the eternity of the highest heights.

Raise your eyes up towards the blue of the sky and consciously tie yourself to the divine spirit, to the Most High, to the Supreme One—with a feeling of elevation, of ennoblement, and of unlimited perfection.

Just as you were able to realize that the earth is carrying you and supporting you, you must also succeed in feeling that the infinite immensity of the sky above you is elevating you, is attracting you upwards, is straightening you up, and is awakening you inside your true eternal being.

The third habit to be acquired consists of feeling yourself to be like a point of liaison between the sky and the earth, allowing the inspirations of the spirit to pass into matter and elevating the energies of matter up towards the spirit.

Whatever he does, an artisan of peace is aware of the earth, of himself and of the spirit, and also of his ability to make the spirit material and to make matter spiritual. For example, when he is eating, he is aware that he is making matter spiritual; and this is why he strives to perform this action with gratitude—inviting in the most elevated thoughts.

When he speaks, he is aware that it is the beauty of the spirit that is being manifested through his words; and he strives, therefore, to build up, and not to destroy. But these examples are poor compared with the profound discoveries waiting for the person who strives to acquire these habits in life. He will see, inside himself, that everything negative can be suppressed, and transformed by the power of the spirit—and that only the awakened man can make it possible for the kingdom of peace to materialize inside the earthly reality, by adopting the new life of the spirit.

Become Aware Of The Ground Which Carries You

The second stage consists of performing the following meditative exercise.

Get into a comfortable position, and enter into a sacred and pure atmosphere.

Make sure that your back is straight and that your body is relaxed. Your breathing is gentle and regular.

You feel that you are in harmony with yourself and with your environment; and you enter progressively into a state of calm and tranquility—and even serenity, if you can.

Then become aware of the ground which is carrying you—of the earth, of matter. Awaken your consciousness to the contact with the ground, as if it were the first time that you were encountering it. Forget everything that you have learned, or that you think you know, and enter into a new relationship with the earth which carries you.

Do the exercise until you can really feel the ground and you understand its meaning inside yourself. To understand does not mean to have a knowledge that is only external and superficial, but to live, internally, an intimate experience with the other thing—in this case, the ground, the matter which makes up the world; let this meeting be transformed into warmth in your heart, then into light in your thoughts—and into an awareness which transforms your life. If one's life is not transformed, then there is no true comprehension in the initiatic sense. Throughout the whole wide world, countless are those who have understood that peace is better than war, that love is better than hatred, that wisdom is better than absurdity; and, yet, they are still the same—unconscious servants of war, of hatred, and of informed ignorance.

For initiates, true knowledge can only be born from love. When I tell you to concentrate on the ground which carries you, don't tense up in relation to it; instead, confidently give the weight of your body over to it. I invite you to fall in love with the earth. If you are not in love, you will not acquire any knowledge. The sacred teaching of the eternal wisdom is for those in love—the valiant hearts, the ardent ones.

It is out of the question to just sit down and concentrate coldly on the ground. Your entire being must participate in the exercise, because it is the entire being that must be transformed. Without the fire of love, no transformation is possible.

Sitting on the ground as I am teaching you to do is dangerous, because you will be transformed. Wanting to approach peace without being ready to transform oneself completely is negative.

The human beings recognized as the most intelligent on the planet have invented all kinds of systems—each one more complicated than the last—for achieving peace on the earth. The teaching of the initiates tells you: if you want to find peace and build its kingdom, begin by becoming aware of the ground which carries you; this is the most powerful method—but only the person who is authentic, pure, and in love with life will be able to put it into practice successfully. Do you see the difference between these two methods—the one coming from the intelligence of the world, and the one coming from eternal wisdom? One must always begin at the beginning, and not put the cart before the horse. Thus, you will have performed the exercise perfectly when, at each stage, you have obtained a new awareness which has the force to transform your relationship with the element being worked upon. This is about establishing new loving relationships with the ground, with yourself, with your own consciousness and with the immensity of the sky.

From another point of view, the ground and the sky represent your mother, who carries you in her abdomen, feeds you, protects you, and offers you all of the best conditions in which to evolve and develop. The sky carries within itself the same idea as your Father, who is the creative source of your life, and the representative of wisdom, of the authority of the holy cosmic law, and of justice. For this reason, we say: *"Our Father, who art in heaven"*. The principle of the father, of the spirit, is tied to a certain awareness of the sky, which human beings have lost. It is the task of the artisan of peace to re-establish this conscious and internal bond with the sky and the earth.

Above You: The Immensity Of The Sky

When, with practice, you have really been able to feel the ground, a state of physical immobility and of inner calm must appear.

Concentrate on the immensity of the sky above you.

Raise yourself up, in your thoughts, towards the highest point that you can imagine; and, when you have reached it, stay there, open up your consciousness to the Sublime, and strive to capture the spirit, and to unite yourself with it.

Unite your thoughts with—and open up your consciousness to—the unlimited, the immense, the infinite, the eternal; then come back down towards your physical body and the consciousness which inhabits it.

If you perform this Johannite exercise correctly, you will perceive that a transformation is taking place inside of you, very gently. New senses of perception are developing, which allow you to enter into contact with realities which had remained invisible to you up to that time. For example, you may perceive that there is another life, another part of yourself, which you did not know about. By concentrating only on your physical body, you have neglected a part of yourself; in addition, inside your body, an earthly self has developed—one which does not include your spiritual side, but lives locked-up inside itself. It is this self that stands in the way of a larger vision of yourself, of the world and of the spirit.

In concentrating on the sky, you have perceived that you have a celestial self which lives in harmony with the spirit, just as the earthly self lives in harmony with the physical body. It is upon the union of these two parts of yourself that peace depends.

Words Of Light On The Law Of Evolution

Meditate deeply upon these words of light until they become perfectly clear for you.

Peace is a fullness, an immobility, a unity.

In unity, everything is contained but nothing is known, since knowledge proceeds from a separation and a comparison. It is in separation that the consciousness is born. Thus, as soon as something separates itself from the original creative unity, it leaves the spirit to appear inside matter. Everything that you see around you is inside you; you identify it because it is separated from the unity.

The spirit is unity.

Matter is diversity and universality.

It is from matter that the consciousness is born, and it is by way of the consciousness that matter can return towards the spirit.

The unity of the spirit manifests itself everywhere and fills everything. It is what pushes all of the separated parts to look for unity once again and, by means of this quest, to produce the movement of life—called "evolution".

The spirit does not evolve; it's not looking for anything, it is not separated. It is all and nothing simultaneously; it is omniscient, omnipresent, omnipotent. It is impossible to add anything whatsoever to the spirit. For it, there is no progress. This is why it is the source of peace.

Matter, on the other hand, evolves. To want to apply peace—immobility—to matter is to create war; this is the source of all suffering.

Those human beings who have lost the vision of the spirit think that evolution leads them towards death, annihilation; so, with all their force, they oppose true progress—the return to the divine unity, to fullness.

Humanity has made enormous progress, but only in the technical and scientific fields—fighting against the spirit and against evolution, by reinforcing the material side, and by hardening it instead of spiritualizing it, instead of making it more subtle. Human beings transform their prison into a fortress—to be sure that they will not be able to escape from their suffering. They trap themselves with ignorance and blindness.

All those who are opposed to the law of evolution are condemned to disappear—because who can fight against life?

Turning towards the spirit and leading matter towards it—by spiritualizing it—is the true evolution. It is the key to peace.

It is impossible to find peace—or fullness or happiness—inside matter, because matter is separated from the spirit and, therefore, does not contain the totality.

How could that which is limited contain the whole? The body of a man cannot contain the ocean. But his consciousness can; that is the secret. Therefore, it is the consciousness which must create peace. Only the one who is peace can know peace. All those who teach that peace can be manufactured outside of oneself—without the participation of the consciousness and the life of the individual—are the enemies of humanity, or are in the service of those enemies, either consciously or unconsciously.

How can an individual's life and consciousness be one with peace? By turning towards the one-spirit, towards God, towards the source—and by merging with him. This is a whole art, a whole science, an entire know-how. Your spirit is already one with the divine spirit—because, since the spirit is one, it lives in all beings and contains all of them, without being contained by any of them. It is indivisible, and present everywhere—filling up everything, from the tiniest atom to immeasurable infinity. It is inside of you at this very moment, because no one can reject the unity without also rejecting himself.

This is what gives life to your body and allows your earthly self to feel separated from the Whole, so that it can live its own life. It is because you identified yourself with your body that the separated self, which you call your personality, appeared. But, in reality, it does not have its own essence; and that is why you are afraid of losing it, afraid of ceasing to exist, and why you hang onto matter so desperately. But, in reality, your personal self is the bride destined to unite herself with the celestial husband—the divine spirit—in order to find peace and the love which triumphs over death. This is the meaning of healthy evolution.

The Great Secret Of Initiation And Peace

Your consciousness appeared because you separated yourself from the unity and constructed a body. Now the consciousness must return towards the unity, and spiritualize the body in order to lead it towards the spirit. In this way, the body becomes the temple of the Most High; it becomes the body of God, the solar body of

Christ. It is the body that must obey the consciousness, and not the consciousness the body; otherwise it is death which triumphs.

The spirit is one, and all beings have the same one; they draw the water of their life from the same unique source. Thus, in attaining the spirit, you become one with all beings.

Being in harmony with all beings—that is peace.

If you know this peace on-high, in the kingdom of the spirit, then you must achieve it down-below, in the kingdom of forms. This is what it means to take up the sword and to be committed to the royal battle against oneself. The body and all of the outer shells must become the receptacle of the spirit. This is the great secret of initiation and of peace. Christ pointed out this secret in his words: *"Heavenly Father, thy will be done, on earth as it is in heaven."* The disciple must raise his consciousness up towards the splendor and the perfection of the spirit; and then he must bring this splendor back down into matter, into his personality and his body.

The whole task of an artisan of peace consists of preparing himself, in all of his outer shells, so that the spirit will be able to come into him and manifest itself in liberty.

The Great Meditation For Peace: The Ground, You, And The Sky

While practicing your concentration on the ground, the sky and yourself, you will perceive that a new light appears inside of you. You will consider the world in a different way—more spiritual, subtle and just.

You will discover an unchangeable, pure and eternal world above you, a world in motion and perpetual transformation below you—and yourself as a mixture of these two realities.

By putting these three worlds in their correct places, you will obtain the order which is the guarantee of peace. Then you can continue the exercise of meditation for peace.

After your concentration on the ground, the sky and yourself, become aware of the ground once again; feel it from inside yourself. Then concentrate on your physical body; feel it, experience it, and, with your imagination, travel all through it—both inside and outside.

Thoughts and images are going to come to you, and you must remain aware, and be the one who observes everything and who directs your concentration onto your body.

If you perform this exercise carefully, you will become aware that all of the particles which make up your body and its organs come from the earth and the universe.

You will feel your body begin to resonate with the whole universe, and even melt into it.

Then pronounce these words of peace:

"Through my body, I awaken.

My body and the universe are one.

It is carried by the earth,

Elevated by the sky of life."

Think it, feel it, live it.

The Great Meditation For Peace: Life

Next, concentrate on the life that fills up the whole earth and animates all beings.

Become aware that nature is alive, and strive to develop the sense of the perception of life. You are entering a new dimension.

Feel how your body is filled with life, and understand the meaning of this life.

Your life is not separated from other lives or from the impersonal one-life.

Life is one, becomes multiple, and returns to the unity.

Let your personal life begin to resonate with the universal one-life and melt into it.

Then pronounce these words of peace:

> "Through life, I awaken.
> My life and the universal life are one.
> It is carried by the earth of the body,
> Elevated by the sky of desire."

Think it, feel it, live it on the inside.

The Great Meditation: The Purification Of Desire

Concentrate on the force of desire which fills up the worlds, animates them and directs them.

Consciously enter the world of desire.

Tell me what your desire is, and I will tell you who your master is, who is directing your life.

Become aware that your own desires are carried by the desires of the world and can be elevated by the kingdom of the spirit. If an ascending direction is not given to one's desires, then they become unconscious and blind, and fate triumphs—to the detriment of the intelligence illuminated by the Holy Spirit.

Desire has its source in the world of the outer shells, of separatism. We always desire what we do not have. Desiring peace shows that we are not at peace, that we are missing something. What do the outer shells aspire to? To be reunited, once again—in the unity of the spirit which brings the fullness of paradise, peace. All desires are born out of this movement towards the divine, towards the eternal—reunification.

Desire must lead towards evolution and must no longer be wasted. All waste is a seed of suffering planted in the internal soil of the soul.

Life is generous and man must be generous; and generosity of heart is not a waste—far from it.

Love is good, love is constructive; it enriches life and makes it more beautiful.

It is the dark, negative, unnecessary and misdirected desires that squander life and lead to every misfortune.

Desire is an immeasurable force which must be directed by the light of the spirit; otherwise, it leads towards degeneration, destruction and slavery.

In your meditation-concentration, strive to put some order into your desires.

First of all, consciously observe your desires without complacency, and under a bright light. Bad desires do not like light, nor do they like to be observed—and this is why they will end up leaving you on their own if you become an observer who projects light.

The awakened consciousness is the observer, and the light proceeds from its union with the Holy Spirit, the cosmic intelligence.

Secondly, consciously sow positive desires and noble aspirations, and especially the great and unique desire to unite yourself once again with the Whole, and the true being that you are eternally—and the only one that will be able to fulfill all of your desires. Know that you will obtain everything that you desire one day—to your joy or to your sorrow, in this life or in another. It is the force of desire that chains man to the wheel of eternally-beginning-again; but it is also this force which leads the wise man towards the sublime goal of unity.

The person who attains celestial unity desires nothing more because he is Whole.

Bad desires are the ones that push you away from your true being in order to lead you into lies, making you believe that you will obtain happiness, peace and good fortune by pursuing external goals—which you will never be able to achieve, and which will never depend on you, anyway. How can a man achieve happiness through external things which he will never be able to grasp hold of or control? A house, a family, wealth and fame are extremely elusive; they do not depend on the man, and can be taken away from him in a split-second.

The wise man understands that he cannot gain possession of anything but himself in the highest heights; and then he possesses the Whole and reigns over the Whole. Everything becomes right and good because he rests inside himself in the divine unity, and nothing bad can come from him ever again. He is a son of God, an artisan of peace.

The person who has not found his treasure of light inside himself looks for it on the outside, around other people; he wants to steal what does not belong to him, and war is inevitable.

The treasure of light is inside of you; don't look for it anywhere else, because you will be deluding yourself, and you will gain nothing from this search.

Man comes into the world naked, and he goes out of it naked.

Go deep into these thoughts in your meditation; then unite all of the force of your desire inside the light of the spirit, of your true being that you are eternally. During the time spent on this exercise, strive to turn the force of your desire inside yourself and to direct it towards the summit of the spirit in such a way that it will no longer flow out of you.

Think of the supreme happiness and the fulfillment that are states of being and of consciousness which we can only live on the inside. Turn your desire towards these—wanting to taste them inside yourself; and leave the outside world behind—forget about it, abandon it for a while.

This is a great secret and a great technique for true peace.

By abandoning the external world in order to elevate himself towards the fullness of the source of the spirit, the disciple enriches himself with treasures which he can then send flowing back out onto the external world.

If all human beings practiced very simple methods like these, the earth would become an extraordinary paradise. Love, peace, joy, respect, liberty, confidence and fulfillment would flow between human beings. The entire atmosphere would be transformed; everything would breathe health, wisdom and love. Everything would be illuminated—in the streets, in the stores; everywhere, love and peace would reign.

Human beings believe that this could only happen in a utopia; and, yet, they do the same thing with the dark and negative side. Now, in the streets of the big cities, we can feel fear, distrust, aggressiveness, coldness, indifference, cowardliness, nastiness and irritability circulating among human beings. So, if it's possible for the negative, why wouldn't it be possible for the positive? All that is required is to simply change methods, and the results will follow. It's mathematical, logical, and scientific.

Yes, human beings all agree that they want what is good-which they no longer know in its true purity-but this is in theory; because, in practice, they want to continue to serve their master—the desire for possession, for glory, for power, etc. They are dark and shadowy because they have made a pact with the darkness; and now they are afraid that the light will make them disappear, and that, in the light, they won't be anything anymore.

They don't want to change; they don't want to transform themselves, or make any effort.

Make the creative force of your desire conscious; turn it towards the inside and direct it upwards—towards the eternal, the timeless.

You unite your desire once again with the original desire of the earth, of the universe which longs to find the divine unity again.

Then pronounce these words of peace:

"Through the driving force of desire, I awaken.

My desire and the desire of the universe are one.

It is carried by the earth of life,

Elevated by the sky of the personality."

Think it, feel it, live it deeply.

The Great Meditation: The Force Of The Will And The Miracle Of The Person

Concerning the world of desire, you must also reflect upon the fact that the force of desire is transformed into the will by passing through the earthly self.

Find the moment when desire changes itself into will.

The will is a force directed by the consciousness. The more your consciousness awakens, the more your will asserts itself and the stronger it grows. The development of the consciousness and that of the will must go hand-in-hand. One must not take the lead over the other. A strong will without consciousness and a luminous consciousness without the will are causes of imbalance and conflict.

The will is a determining agent in life because it is tied to the driving force of desire. Like desire, it must be put at the service of the consciousness united with the spirit.

"Not my will, but thy will be done, heavenly Father-Mother."

The Father-Mother is the highest consciousness that a being can attain. It is where the source of the being—therefore, the true being—resides. The person whose actions originate in his true being is authentic and, therefore, free.

Whereas the person whose actions originate in the will of the earthly self is a prisoner and a slave. It is not him acting—but the world and the person born of the world that are acting inside of him.

If, deep-down inside, you ask yourself questions about these words, and if you perform the meditative exercise correctly, you will be able to become aware of the fact that you are not your body, and not your life—nor your desires or your will.

The body appeared as a receptacle of the spirit because, otherwise, it could not manifest itself. By contrasting with the spirit, the body allows it to appear. Life came to vivify the body. Desire came to lead it onto the path of evolution through experiences. Desire wants to lead the body towards the spirit; this is the road of return and of fulfillment.

The will endows the body with a personality, a self which reflects the image of the sovereign spirit. This personality is born of the body, and, therefore, it carries the mark of separation; it is not yet the pure receptacle, the perfect image of the spirit, the bride prepared for the wedding.

The more the development progresses, the closer matter comes to the spirit, the more it is refined and spiritualized, and acquires superior faculties. But, despite these faculties, it is still separated, and man still does not know himself in truth; he has not reached the supreme goal—unity, the king, the I-Am, the Father-Mother.

Retaining the subtle essence of these words, concentrate on the personality which appears in the first movement of the will.

Become aware of the personality acting everywhere in the world and in the universe to individualize all of the particles coming out of the primary source.

Feel your own personality, which carries your self. Perceive how your personality was formed by the forces of the cosmos—the earth—and by the great personality.

Let your personality begin to resonate with the great personality and melt into it.

In this way, you will be able to understand the words of the Cosmic Tradition: *"Every man contains all men."*

You yourself contain every personality, and you can wear each one of them—like a series of masks.

The source of all illusion comes from this world of desire, and from the personality emanating from it. Becoming autonomous, this personality is able to fight against the spirit and to rebel against the celestial order—which confirms these words of wisdom:

"War is always internal before being external." Suppress the ancient internal conflict and the external conflict disappears.

The personality separated from its celestial spouse and fighting against it in order to assert itself, not knowing itself who it is—this is the source of all war.

Therefore, do not tense up inside your personality or your will; instead, relax and recognize that you are carrying all personalities.

The seed of the personality resides in the separation of the body, which generates illusion and selfishness.

Its fulfillment is in the union with the spirit.

Meditate deeply upon this, because the source of true knowledge is inside of you.

Then pronounce these words of peace:

"Through my will and my personality, I awaken.

My personality and the great personality are one.

My person is carried by the earth of desire,

Elevated by the sky of the heart.

I Am the bride prepared for the wedding of the lamb."

Think it, feel it, live it intensely.

The Great Meditation: The Elevation Of The Heart

Concentrate on your heart—on the soul of feeling and sensitivity.

Obviously, each new concentration must be tied to the preceding one. There is a progression, an evolution, a spiritualization, which manifests itself through the exercise. The physical body appears in the bosom of the earth; it is raised up towards the spirit by life—which is itself carried by the body and raised up towards desire, etc. Thus, the heart appears in the personality. If the personality is not united with the bride—still virginal and correctly prepared—then the heart will not be pure, but monopolized by the sensitivity of the personality.

Centered inside your own heart, strive to elevate yourself all the way up to the purity of the heart by inviting into it feelings that are noble, beautiful, good, unselfish and mystical.

Through the sensitivity of your own heart, plunge yourself into the sensitivity of the world. Your own soul of feeling is born out of the feeling of the world.

If you perform your concentrations in the right way, you should perceive that, indeed, the world is filled with feeling, imagination, sympathy-antipathy, etc. But, among all of these feelings, all of these personalities, and all of these lives in motion, there are some with which you do not wish to unite, because you judge them to be negative, sick, dark, etc.

A desire for protection may then rise up inside of you; and it's true that protection is necessary. This protection resides in the fact of you truly being yourself. Fear must never be a guide; love is the true guide.

The person who is centered inside himself has the choice, and he can separate what is good for him from what is not. It is precisely in this selection that peace resides. If you put just any food into your physical body, you will get sick—and you might even die. For the body, peace resides in good health, and war in illness. Illness appears because the body has been placed in a current that is not healthy for it, which prevents it from functioning properly and hinders its evolution. We have seen that the healthy evolution of the body is life. The person who does not raise his body up towards life does not enter the ascending current and, therefore, struggles against the natural evolution. This illustrates a law which applies to everything—and the more we progress, the more disorder becomes established; if disharmony moves into the relationship between the earth and the physical body, then it will expand into life, desire, the will, the personality, the heart, etc. Everything falls into anarchy.

So you can feel two currents during your concentration:
- An anarchical current of an unhealthy evolution.
- A synarchical current of a harmonious and healthy evolution.

You can also discern two humanities:

- A dark, unconscious humanity.
- A luminous, conscious humanity.

When Christ talked about building his church on the rock and not on the sand, he was referring to these two humanities.

The humanity of light is the School of Christ. It builds on rock, because, for each floor, there is a solid foundation and a clearly indicated elevation.

Man's body must rest on the ground and push its roots down into it. It is itself an elevation, a spiritualization, of the earth and of the cosmos.

The body must be raised up into life, which pushes its own roots deep into it.

Life is raised up into desire, etc.

The dark humanity doesn't even know anymore what the body is supposed to rest upon; it no longer has any roots or orientation. Having lost the meaning of everything, it is dispossessed of its being, and heading towards death, destruction and degeneration.

In your meditation, these two currents must come before you; and you must not reject either one, because they both live in your soul. They must simply be balanced and put in their respective places. You must unite yourself intimately with the current of light, and leave the dark current outside of yourself—and even behind you. This current will then become positive because it will awaken you by showing you clearly what you must not do. There is an impure heart and a pure heart. You must expel what renders the heart impure and the sensitivity inhuman; and you must not let it enter you again. What purifies the heart must be invited in and strengthened.

"Blessed are the pure of heart for they shall see God."

God is everywhere; the person who sees the beautiful, the true, the good, the just and the luminous, everywhere and in everything, has a pure heart.

In his Apocalypse, the Master St. John uses some analogous images to describe the personality. First, it's *"the hardened prostitute who puts herself at the service of the beast"*, and then it's *"the bride prepared for the wedding of the lamb."*

Let the one who has ears hear, and let the one who has eyes contemplate the mysteries of the creation and of initiation.

The person who cannot discern these two currents inside himself and in the world is a prisoner of the darkness; he cannot work for peace. He needs to be struck by the sword, to be split in two, and to acquire the true intelligence of the heart.

So when I say to you: "With your heart, plunge yourself into the sensitivity of the world," it's not to weaken you, but to awaken you with more sharpness inside your own sensitivity. The same holds true for the personality. Being one with the personality of the world does not mean that you lose your own personality; on the contrary, you gain it. If you are one with the personality of the world, it becomes dangerous; you are obliged to awaken and to choose the best currents. You must ask yourself this question: "What is the origin, the reality, and the final goal of the personality, of the heart, and of life?"

You have to find yourself on your own and get into harmony with the Whole in a new way.

The path of peace is not the easy path. Opening up your heart is not easy. It takes a lot of courage. It almost requires that you be a hero.

Peace is a heroic and chivalrous path. Deciding to work for the authentic peace is a glorious exploit.

Concentrate on your heart; plunge its roots deep into the purified personality. Clearly discern the bad influences which monopolize the heart; and make the decision to raise your heart up towards the heights, towards the sacred and divine.

Become aware that your heart is not separated from other hearts or from the sensitivity of the universe. Love is the right atmosphere for the authentic heart. The pure heart is the door to the universal soul.

Let your heart begin to resonate with the universal love and to melt in it.

Then pronounce these words of peace:

> "Through my heart, I awaken.
> My heart and the universal heart are one.
> It is carried by the earth of the personality,
> Elevated by the sky of the thoughts."

Think it, feel it, live it completely.

The Great Meditation: The Mastery Of The Thoughts

Concentrate on your own ability to think.

Think consciously: "I am thinking."

Awaken to the fact that the earth is filled with thoughts and, especially, with wisdom.

The current of dark and absurd thoughts proceeds from humanity; but, in the cosmos, everything is wisdom.

Feel how wonderful the ability to think is; it allows you to travel through space, to communicate with the invisible world, to receive a higher knowledge, to unite yourself with immortal, celestial ideas, and to create a work of light—or a work of darkness.

You think of peace as of an eternal idea—alive on its own; and, through your thoughts, you unite yourself with it and receive its celestial vibration.

Become aware that your thoughts are not separated from the thoughts of the world. Your body itself is a crystallized thought. Everything is a thought, everything is wisdom—the light of the cosmic intelligence.

Let your thoughts begin to resonate with the cosmic intelligence and melt into it.

Then pronounce these words of peace:

"Through my thoughts, I awaken.

My thoughts and the cosmic intelligence are one.

> They are carried by the earth of the heart,
> Elevated by the sky of eternity."

Think it, feel it, live it in the spirit.

The Great Meditation: The Eternal "I"

Concentrate on the eternity which fills up the world, maintains it, and guides it towards a mysterious goal.

Become aware that, behind the ephemeral appearances, there stands eternity.

Eternity in motion—that is evolution. Everything revolves around the eternal spirit, with the goal of melting into it. The sacred teaching is eternal; the sky and the earth move, but not one atom of the cosmic teaching changes. It remains eternally identical to itself. It is the very law of life, which is the model for creation.

In your meditation, find what is eternal in the world and what is eternal in you. Nothing in the world can disappear; everything is transformed. This is the first law of reincarnation, of transformation, of evolution.

Next, there is something which does not change, but which rests eternally inside itself. Find this thing inside yourself and in the world.

Concentrate on your "I ray"—on the highest essence of your I, of yourself—and find this same I-Am throughout the world. Yes, the words "I-Am" resonate in the world. Find your eternal I and you will meet the Master who will guide you towards the highest presence of the sovereign spirit.

Feel how eternity gives a meaning to life.

Let your "I ray", source of the consciousness, begin to resonate with the cosmic eternity and melt into it.

Then pronounce these words of peace:

> "Through eternity, I awaken.
> My "I" and eternity are one.
> It is carried by the earth of the thoughts,
> Elevated by the sky of omniscience."

Think it, feel it, live it in the silence.

The Great Meditation: The Original Gnosis And The Land Of Light

Concentrate on the omniscience, the direct knowledge, the original gnosis. (1)

---

(1) In the Tibetan tradition, this experience is called the ascension into the land of Shamballa. In the Egyptian-Christian tradition, Manisola designates the vision of the celestial Jerusalem that St. John describes in his Apocalypse or manual of initiation. (Editor's Note).

Become aware that the source of knowledge is inside you and outside of you.

Behind eternity appears the omniscience. Then you can see the land of light appear, and the sun of the Mani rising inside of you.

This is an indescribable experience, and it is not necessary to give a lot of information about these stages, because it is by living them that one acquires an exact knowledge of them.

This omniscience is linked to the disciple's commitment to the work for the cosmic hierarchy, which is the celestial order—visible and invisible. If the disciple does not accomplish the task assigned to him by the one-spirit, then he cannot gain access to the omniscience, because he would be crushed by the knowledge that he would receive from it, and he would become unusable and, therefore, useless.

On the path of harmonious evolution and, therefore, of peace, all knowledge must be applied in life; otherwise, it penetrates into the domain of death—dragging the disciple along with it.

In order to gain access to the omniscience, one has to have already mastered and consolidated the preceding stages. Transforming living knowledge into dead knowledge is forbidden to the initiate of this degree. The work of the disciple of peace is to vivify dead knowledge and transform it into living knowledge through application. It is the spirit that vivifies.

Let your intuitive spiritual perception begin to resonate with the omniscience of the spirit and melt into it.

Then pronounce these words of peace:

> "Through omniscience, I awaken.
> My column of intuition and the divine omniscience are one.
> It is carried by the earth of eternity,
> Elevated by the sky of omnipresence."

Think it, feel it, live it in the spirit.

The Great Meditation: The Omnipresence Of The Holy Spirit

Concentrate on the omnipresence of the spirit in the world and in the universe.

Awaken to the thought that there is not one place in the infinite cosmos where the spirit is not present. Everywhere you look, it is there.

It is inside you—in each one of the components of your being, in each one of your cells.

You can unite yourself to it and be everywhere at the same time—to such an extent that you will no longer be able to tell the difference between here and there.

Behind the omniscience stands the omnipresence. Concentrate on this omnipresence of the Holy Spirit and you will find universal love and, in it, the jewel of your soul—one with the soul of souls.

Let your infinite soul begin to resonate with the omnipresence and melt into it.

Then pronounce these words of peace:

> "Through the omnipresence of the Holy Spirit, I awaken.
> My soul and the omnipresence are one.
> It is carried by the earth of omniscience,
> Elevated by the sky of omnipotence."

Think it, feel it, live it in the Holy Spirit.

The Great Meditation: The Force Of The Holy Spirit Is The Only Force

Concentrate on the power and the creative force of the primary source of the spirit.

The entire universe is sustained by the omnipotence of the Holy Spirit.

Universal love is the supreme law which guides this creative force. In the divine will is expressed the highest love—the gift of oneself, sacrifice. The Divinity offers itself to all beings to be shared, so that all may participate in the mysteries of the Being.

The person who, in full consciousness, offers himself to the Being of beings in purity will find the treasure of light and will reign over the Whole.

Become aware of the force which directs the progression of the worlds and protects all of the paths of destiny.

Awaken to the great reality of the cosmic order.

There is an order inside of you, too—a harmony which must succeed in reflecting the cosmic order.

Then you will understand that *"there is no force like the force of the Holy Spirit; only the force of the Holy Spirit is the force of God."* (1)

This omnipotence of the Holy Spirit, emanating from the cosmic unison, is also inside of you; and it is, precisely, inside yourself that you must find it. The person who does not make any effort cannot be helped. Therefore, you can feel inside yourself the presence of the force which allows you to undertake everything and to succeed in everything; but always be conscious that it does not come from you, but from the source of the Holy Spirit. It is offered to you as a gift, and it is up to you to make it grow through glorious actions.

The omnipotence hides behind the omnipresence in the sky of the spirit. In it, you find your own spirit, which is one with the great spirit. You perceive that you have never been separated from the divine spirit and that you have always accomplished its will; but you had forgotten this, because you were living only in your body and your earthly personality. Having detached yourself from your

---

(1) These are mantric words from the Master Peter Deunov (Beinsa Douno). (Author's Note.)

coarser nature, you enter the domain of the pure spirit; and you understand, you live these words: *"The heavenly Father and I are one."* Not only are you one with the spirit; you are also already working with it for the good of all of the beings everywhere in the cosmos. At this moment, in the earthly reality of your body, you are not conscious of this mystery; but this unconsciousness absolutely does not prevent the fact from occurring. Even if you are unconscious of the beating of your heart, it still continues to beat.

Your spirit is already one with the Supreme One; it is omnipotent, omnipresent, omniscient. It is participating in the life of the cosmos and in the work of creation—but you don't know it, because your consciousness is imprisoned inside your physical body. The first thing to do is to re-establish the bond with the spirit by working on yourself. When this bond is re-established, then you must come back down into your physical body and your earthly self in order to purify them, to strengthen them—and to render them capable of receiving, and of working in harmony with, the high vibrations of the spirit.

Therefore, this meditation has two parts:

- The first one consists of becoming aware of the outer shells of the being, of bringing them into harmony with one another, and then of detaching oneself from them in order to rise up into the higher vibration—until one reaches the source of the spirit.

- The second consists of receiving the force of the spirit in order to accomplish all of the work of self-transformation inside the body and the earthly personality.

The force of the spirit offers you the possibility to transform yourself and, in this way, to improve the world.

Become aware that only the person who has transformed himself for the sake of good can accomplish the same thing with the world. He becomes an artisan of peace.

Only a son of God—the person who has found the force of the spirit—can be an artisan of peace. First, inside himself, through his own transformation—and then in the world. You must not wait for the transformation and the work to come from other people, from the outside world—because, if you do, then liberty is lost.

One must become free through one's own force, in harmony with the Good of the Whole.

The key is that you must understand that you do not need to transform the spirit, because it is already perfect—like the heavenly Father. The kingdom of free peace is already a reality; all you have to do is invite it into yourself and give it the best conditions, so that it can incarnate.

It is the body and the earthly personality that must be transformed and educated, in order to become receptacles, revelations, instruments of the spirit.

The body and the spirit must come together and merge in order to give birth to the Christ-like consciousness inside the human being, and to turn him or her into a son or daughter of God.

In the whirlwind of daily life, you can do this exercise: while going about your business, stop for a few seconds and analyze your state of consciousness and of life—which will surely be limited to whatever you are doing.

In the evening, find a tranquil moment to meditate. At that time, bring before your consciousness all of those little stops during the day; and, in your thoughts, elevate yourself towards your spirit, in order to also participate in its cosmic work.

Through this exercise, you will perceive that your consciousness participates in several levels of life. There is the life of your body, your personal life, your work, your family life, your social life, urban life, national life, the life of the world—and, also, the cosmic life.

Well, if you want to find peace, then you have to become a citizen of the universe and consciously participate in life for the Whole—that is, become a Sister or a Brother of the great universal fraternity of the Good without shadows, servants of the cosmic order.

In the silence and immobility, concentrate on the force of the sovereign spirit, and unite your own force to its force.

Let your creative force begin to resonate with the cosmic order and melt into it.

Then pronounce these words of peace:

> "Through the force of the spirit, I awaken.
>
> My heavenly Father and I are one.
>
> He works; and I, too, work—one in Him.
>
> My force is carried by the earth of omnipresence,
>
> Elevated by the sky of the source of the spirit."

Think it, feel it, live it—one with the spirit.

The Great Meditation: The Unmanifested

Concentrate on the "unmanifested" which is beyond all perception and which appears constantly through the manifestations of creation.

The "unmanifested" contains within itself everything possible; it is the supreme unity, the source of peace.

Inside of it is your true eternal being. It is similar to a total silence, a perfect immobility, an entire fullness. You can never find it in the limited, manifested world because it is unlimited, without form, not created: "Unmanifested".

Concentrate on that which is nothing and which contains the Whole—on that which is before the first word, the first breath, the first thought, the first movement, the first beginning.

You cannot do anything without it, because it is everything—and even more than that.

Throughout time, the initiates have named this reality: God, the supreme Being. The Master St. John refers to him in his gospel: *"The beginning of all things lies in the first creative manifestation, the first word. This word was in God, in the silence, in the unmanifested. It was one with Him; it was Him before manifesting itself. Everything was manifested by it; and, without it, nothing was."*

Become aware that, before every word, there is silence, and that each word is as if grafted onto the silence. It is, above all, the silence which gives its full dimension to the word.

The one and the other are inseparable; they represent the two poles of the same unique reality.

Now, if the word returns to the silence, one could believe that it has disappeared; but no—because, between it and the silence, there is an entire hierarchy, and it is through this hierarchy that the word becomes conscious of itself.

The unconscious word generates war.

The conscious word produces peace.

The word becomes conscious of itself starting at the moment when it considers its origin—the great silence. This is when it discovers the thought which gives it life. Behind every word, there is a thought.

Behind the thought comes the verb—the eternal idea which gives life to thoughts.

Behind the idea comes the creative source of the spirit, which bursts forth from the silence and fills up the world.

So the word doesn't disappear; it becomes conscious, and this is the great secret of life: the consciousness can unite all of the opposites in creation and reconstitute the divine unity.

The word and the silence are two opposites, because one is unlimited and the other limited. Only the consciousness allows what is limited to merge with the unlimited, what is divided to know and to be unity.

All of the words uttered in the world will go on confronting one other until they have recognized their common origin and destinations, as well as the unique vibration which unites them—the silence, the unsaid.

When a word is separated from the thought, the idea and the silence, it becomes like the leaf detached from the tree: death is its destiny.

Understand that you are a living word, and that it is only by finding your origin once again that you will discover who you are, and that all duality will flee from you.

Therefore, don't be satisfied just with the dead side of life or with one-half of yourself; instead, try to find the totality—your fullness, your divine unity—once again.

In the immobility of your body and in the silence of your person, elevate your consciousness above your body and your person in order to enter the unmanifested and to merge with the true being which you are for all eternity—and which is the true being of all beings.

Let your consciousness open up inside Him, as the flower opens up in the sun, and you will know what no word will ever be able to express. How could what is limited pronounce the unlimited, the absolute, the infinite?

Then pronounce these words of peace:

"I-Am the unmanifested, the Nothing-Everything.

I am one with the source of all beings.

I am the supreme union of the earth and of the sky of the spirit.

I am love, wisdom and truth.

I am the resurrection and the life."

The Living Tradition

Thus ends the first part of this great meditation for peace. This is an extremely powerful method for finding and creating peace. It emanates from the most ancient traditions of light and from the current of the humanity of St. John.

It is time for humanity—and, more particularly, western civilization—to go back to its roots and rediscover the origins of its culture and its traditions of light. Contained therein are treasures for building peace, for finding happiness, and for living in joy.

Traditions are not kept alive exclusively in cooking recipes and in the art of baking the perfect pie—as they want us to believe.

We must develop a new respect for our ancestors, and carry their light and their aspiration towards the Most High. In this way, each individual takes part in the transmission of the living tradition.

This meditation was taken from the secret and oral tradition so that human beings could understand it, and would reflect upon the fact that the living, initiatic Christianity is not dead, and that very few people on the earth have knowledge of it.

Thus, this meditation contains an entire teaching, and it is not possible to go into it more deeply within this framework—as each of you can surely understand. At a particular moment, the student must pass on to a superior stage of work, and, at that time, he will meet up with the School of St. John, through those who represent it on the earth, to be guided in a more particular and precise way.

The Tree of Peace

I have inserted some explanations into this meditation and these exercises, and I advise the person who really wants to practice them to carefully copy the different parts onto a sheet of paper—keeping only the practical part.

Here, again, is some advice:

It is fundamental to begin with the basic exercises and to wait until they are perfectly mastered before going on to the next stage. It is almost impossible to accomplish the exercise the first time, in just one attempt.

The exercise is based on this law:

>There is something which carries,
>which is carried,
>which elevates.

Peace is like a tree. The man who wants to find peace must also become a tree. If he has no roots and if he does not aspire to raise himself up towards the sky, he will not be able to find peace.

What are your roots?

Who are you?

What is your orientation?

You must answer these three questions; but don't be satisfied just to give a ready-made, manufactured, superficial answer. Peace is not possible without depth.

Man must once again find his roots, his origin, his divine affiliation, and become part of the current of the evolution of light. Only then will peace be able to flow from man and flood the world with its celestial vibration.

This will be the apparition:

- of a new earth,

- of a new humanity,

- of a new sky.

The new man—the man who is the artisan of peace—must plunge his roots into a new earth and want to raise himself up towards a new sky.

The external earth and sky are only the reflection of an internal earth and sky which each person possesses inside himself. The way in which human beings consider the external sky and earth clearly shows that they have abandoned the internal ones.

In reality, every individual has received, as an inheritance, an internal earth to cultivate and a sky to illuminate. The person who loses contact with this earth and this sky on the inside is no longer united with his ancestors. He loses the thread of the living Tradition; he is uprooted and no longer has any direction. He becomes a madman—wandering around haphazardly, having lost his senses.

It is through a new contact with the ground and a new conception of the earth that you can rediscover your internal earth. The same holds true for the sky.

The earth and the sky are alive and must be respected and considered as such. Do not let these words be transformed into a dead theory for you. They are life, and want to carry the new life.

You have to feel how the roots of your body plunge into the earth. If your body is consciously united with the earth, it becomes strong. The earth and your body are one. This is a bond of life, of love and of intelligence which has to be forged.

Stability, food, water, air, light, sounds—all of these awaken you to life, through your body. Become aware; don't be dead.

The earth itself is carried and elevated by the spirit through several levels, of which you are a part.

Your body plunges its roots into the earth and orients itself towards life.

The current circulates between the earth, the body, and life.

Your life plunges its roots into your body and elevates itself through desire.

The current circulates between the body, life, and desire.

Your desire plunges its roots into life and elevates itself in the personality.

The current circulates between life, desire, and the personality.

The personality plunges its roots into the earth of desire and elevates itself through the heart.

The current circulates between desire, the personality, and the heart.

The heart plunges its roots into the earth of the personality and elevates itself in the thoughts.

The current circulates between the personality, the heart, and the thoughts.

The thoughts plunge their roots into the earth of the heart and orient themselves towards eternity.

The current circulates between the heart, the thoughts, and eternity.

Eternity plunges its roots into the earth of the thoughts and elevates itself through the omniscience.

The current circulates between the thoughts, eternity, and the omniscience.

The omniscience plunges its roots into the earth of eternity and elevates itself through the omnipresence.

The current circulates between eternity, the omniscience, and the omnipresence.

The omnipresence plunges its roots into the earth of omniscience and elevates itself towards the omnipotence.

The current circulates between the omniscience, the omnipresence, and the omnipotence.

The omnipotence plunges its roots into the omnipresence and elevates itself into the unmanifested.

The current circulates between the omnipresence, the omnipotence, and the unmanifested.

The unmanifested is immutable, eternally identical to itself.

It plunges its roots into the manifested and elevates it.

The current which circulates through these twelve receptacles of life must be one, and must tie everything together within the unity—just as the sap which circulates in the tree is one, from its roots to its top.

If the current of life which unites matter to the spirit is disturbed in just one place, then peace cannot be found—much less achieved.

Accomplish this work with sincerity and you will find peace.

To reinforce himself, the disciple can ask himself the following questions:

What is the earth and what is matter?

What is the body?

What is life?

What is desire?

What is the personality?

What is the heart?
What are thoughts?
What is eternity?
What is omniscience?
What is omnipresence?
What is omnipotence?
What is the unmanifested?

THE RESPONSE OF THE ETERNAL

What does a man do when he is crushed by suffering?

He looks for a quiet place where he can isolate himself from the world and raises his prayer towards the Most High, in the hope of receiving help and comfort.

What does the wise man do when he aspires to commune with the source of life?

He breaks away from the vibration of the worries of the world, covers himself with the cloak of silence, plunges himself into his inner life, and raises his thoughts towards the Most High.

The answer is always the same—cosmic peace.

The first manifestation of the Supreme is always peace.

Celestial peace is a door which allows one to contemplate the kingdom of the eternal light. Without it, no divine manifestation, no progress, no evolution is possible.

It is always through peace that the Eternal speaks to humanity, gives his help, and renews his alliance.

THE KINGDOM OF PEACE IS LIKE AN EMIGRANT

The kingdom of peace is like an emigrant who is obliged to go to another country to earn money, in order to provide for his family's needs. During his moments of despair, he telephones his wife and children, and gets new strength from them.

In truth, I say to you, man is an emigrant in this world, and that is why he finds pain in it. Through prayer and the elevation of his thoughts towards the heavens, he can establish a bond with his original country and, in this way, gain new strength, experience joy, and find a meaning for his life on earth. Then, thanks to this bond, everything becomes more beautiful, and the worst difficulties can be overcome with force and enrichment. The person who thinks that he is going to make a success of his life on earth without establishing a bond with the land of his soul is drowning in error and illusion—but, very often, it will be too late when he finally sees this.

THE CONSCIOUSNESS OF EXCHANGES: A KEY FOR PEACE

The Communion With The Universe

Become conscious of the many exchanges that you can have with the divine, the living nature, and your inner world; then, direct these exchanges towards the sublime, and you will know peace.

Peace comes from working on oneself, from a discipline in all exchanges, from a selection.

The person who agrees to have exchanges with just anyone and who allows just anything to come inside him cannot find peace, or happiness, or freedom.

There is no peace without an awakened consciousness and there is no awakening of the consciousness without exchange.

Meditate very deeply upon the fact that, in order to live and develop, every organism, every individual, must be in contact with the Whole.

This contact may be conscious or unconscious; but, if it disappears or if it is deficient, the individual falls ill and dies.

In human beings, this contact with the Whole, this union, this communion, must be conscious.

If you want to be an artisan of peace, an authentic man, you must feel yourself in communion with the universe and with all beings.

The whole task of a human being is to re-establish the bond which unites his consciousness to the Divine and to his cosmic environment, both near and far. This is when his life will take on a sublime meaning; everything will be put into order and will become intense. Intense life is a key for peace, because only the divine spirit can give you an intense, exciting, celestial life—one which has a meaning and a universal usefulness.

If you never unite your consciousness with the divine spirit, the sublime love, the highest wisdom, you will never find the meaning of things, and you will remain forever imprisoned inside the external conditions.

Joy and peace reside in conscious, living, pure, celestial, sacred exchanges—which you can have through nature and the Holy Spirit. Such exchanges awaken your inner life, and make you more intelligent, more loving, stronger and more luminous.

Those who constantly find their nourishment in garbage cans and cesspools, and who leave their consciousness and their inner life unused, will never know peace.

Become aware that, through a simple source—a flower, an insect, a tree, the flight of a bird, the face of a child, the wisdom of an old man—you can unite yourself and commune with celestial forces and influences. For this, all you need to do is to love the Most High through everything, and to desire to awaken your inner life and to unite yourself to him.

Only union with the Source, through everything, results in free peace.

The Two Paths Of The Consciousness

The meaning of life, the meaning of everything you do and achieve—even the meaning of what seems like the most insignificant act—is to find this peace which is the fullness of life and of the spirit.

The most insignificant act is part of an uninterrupted chain of influences which must lead you towards this treasure of light—either by a detour of suffering, or by the direct route of purity and light.

Become aware of all of the exchanges that you have in a single day; awaken yourself to a higher dimension through them, and find their hidden meaning.

Two paths will then open up before you:

One leads you towards mindlessness, illness, conflicts and annihilation.

The other leads you towards enrichment, awakening, the soul, intense life, the Most High, success, the sacred teaching, eternity, fullness, supreme Good, service, and totality.

Can you see that these two paths are found in your way of looking at life, the world and yourself—and then in the way that you behave with regard to life, the world and yourself?

The Experiment In A Public Park

Try this experiment of going into a public park and watching the people strolling on the paths in the midst of the tall trees.

Some, lost in their thoughts and worries, do not see the trees.

Others, who have come there to rest and regenerate, unconsciously soak up the peaceful atmosphere created by the majestic aura of the tall trees. Perhaps they will place themselves in the shade of their foliage and experience a feeling of contentment in doing so.

Is there, maybe, one person who is going to marvel at the beauty of a tree? This feeling of amazement awakens his inner life and leads him towards a higher degree of life; but he is not aware of this.

Do this experiment yourself: consciously approach a tree with the intention of meeting its spirit of light through its form. Awaken to the meaning of a tree, to its usefulness with regard to life, to its message and mystical symbolism.

Approach it with the idea that it is a living, sensitive, intelligent being (because intelligence can manifest itself in other forms than just those known to humanity); and be ready to offer it all of your love, your purest and most beneficent intention, all the best of yourself.

Approach it until you are touching it with your hands. Speak to it internally: "O tree, I greet you with my heart, and, through you, I greet all trees and the creator of the universe. I wish you all the best; I would like to become solid and stable, like you, and raise myself up towards the sun. You have my friendship; be at peace."

Remain a few moments in communion with it; then continue walking. You will feel transformed and vivified.

Of course, there are different ways to commune with a tree.

First, with your body; this is basic, but one must recognize that the exchanges confined to the body are quite weak.

With your life, you can feel an energy leaving you to go into the tree, and another one flowing from the tree into you

With your heart and the sensitivity of your soul, for example, you can marvel at the size and the strength of a tree. This creates a particular feeling inside of you.

With your thoughts, you can receive an entire internal teaching from a tree. There are Master-Trees.

A Disciple Must Unite Himself With The Sublime Spirit Which Soars Above Creation

The more you remain locked-up inside your physical body, the more limited you are, the poorer your life becomes, and the more your soul falls asleep. Whereas the more you raise yourself up towards exchanges on-high, in the spheres of the spirit, the more your life becomes enriched, expanded, and intensified—approaching fullness—and the more you are purified, inspired, vivified and illuminated. Everything inside of you is put back into place, and peace appears.

Yes, only the Holy Spirit, the celestial communion between man and his eternal being, can achieve peace. Do you understand this?

Every being must once again find the path of the sublime spirit which soars above creation, and re-establish a conscious bond with it. You must have experiences on your own, and stop having exchanges only on the lower level, unconsciously; instead, you must begin to nourish your soul and your spirit through your exchanges.

Human beings attract every negative state into themselves; they unleash hell, and ignore the celestial states which generate peace, harmony, intelligence, and mastery. And then they are amazed to find themselves plunged into torment, war, atrocities, tears, and gnashing of teeth.

If you invite the force of Good-without-shadows inside yourself, it will build the kingdom of peace, and you will find your treasure of light—which will make you a king.

If you invite the influences of good-mixed-with-evil, they will lead you into slavery, will reduce you to mindlessness, will deprive you of the light of your being, will destroy everything inside of you, and will annihilate you.

If human beings no longer see the spiritual kingdom which lives above them and inside of them, it is because they have invited in the dark forces and have put themselves under their control. Thus, these forces have blocked their spiritual vision, and have put a seal over the eye of their intelligence—so effectively that they do not know anymore what is good and what is bad. They have lost the meaning of life; they are lost, and are blindly allowing themselves to be guided by those who are leading them to the slaughterhouse.

The man who gives up his intelligence and allows others to guide his life is no longer a human being. Anyone can get him to do just anything.

War—with its murders, its rape, its pillaging, its destruction—isn't that just anything?

How many people are for peace, but still allow themselves to be carried away by the crashing wave of war? It is not enough just to be for peace; one must become strong, in order to resist being carried away by the influences of war. True force is found only in the communion with the spirit. The person who has merged with the spirit of light in a state of superior consciousness has contemplated the meaning of life; he has become capable of understanding the teaching of the initiates, and never again can anything shake him up or make him change his mind. He has decided to put himself at the service of good and has rejected the lies.

True good does not want evil. In it, everything is good and everything works for what is good. The very energy of evil is transformed, channeled and directed towards the goal of what is good.

Only the person who has understood the meaning of life can transform evil into good, because he has received the illumination of the spirit. This illumination is available to all those who want to receive it and who are ready to make an effort to achieve it.

Only the spirit can confer it, and will only do so for those who are ready to receive it. So the meaning of life—just like peace—cannot be given or manufactured by man, because it is identical to itself. It is up to man to receive it in purity and to conform to it.

The Disciple's Experience With A Master-Tree

And now, to make things even clearer, here is an experience which a sincere disciple can have by approaching and communing with a Master-Tree.

He touches the tree and unites himself with it through his awakened inner life. After a while, he feels a kind of shiver going through him from head to toe; a light-energy has just run through his body. His spiritual eyes have opened, and he sees this energy as a dancing fire going up and down the entire tree. All of the leaves, the branches and the roots are one unity through the means of this fire which rises up towards the heights of the sky and plunges into the depths of the earth. There is something very mysterious about all of this—which is why the tree has always been venerated by people close to nature and life.

Then the disciple sees that this tree is not isolated from other trees, but that they are communicating with one another all over the planet, through a means still unknown to man—even though they also live inside of him, by way of his heart.

There are, so to speak, threads of light which go from the tree towards other trees, and also towards certain places—certain mountaintops or valleys—and even towards certain human beings. Thus, there are human beings who are in constant communication with trees. Their inner life is nourished by the inspiration of trees.

Of course, I cannot go into the details, but here is the thing—surprising and full of meaning—that a disciple sees: in fact, the currents of light which unite the tree to other trees, and to many other places and beings, are beneficent, vivifying influences. But other currents appear before his eyes—ones which are dead, negative, hateful, dark. These currents fill up space and are themselves also tied to certain places, summits, valleys, rocks, sick trees, human beings, and animals—which are their transmitters-receivers. Thus, just as there is a union, a solidarity, a brotherhood, for what is good, there is also one for what is evil. It was to explain this vision of a disciple that the holy scriptures of humanity talked about the tree of the knowledge of good and evil.

So there are places, objects, and human beings which are transmitters-receivers, amplifiers, of evil, of war, of lies, of atrocities. As soon as someone has a dark, negative thought, he attracts these currents to himself and they suck up his thought. This thought travels through space, and will be stored in places which form the energy-reserve of evil. It is these reservoirs that are used by negative people to fire up crowds, to manipulate them, and to lead them towards war and destruction. These reservoirs are constantly being restocked with all of the unhappiness—all of the negative feelings, thoughts, desires and actions—of human beings. Thus, through their unconscious way of living, human beings are working towards their own downfall, and are the agents of evil on the earth.

This is why it is necessary to learn how to fill up the reservoirs of good, of true peace, of the teaching of the universal man. The School of St. John is one of these reservoirs; it is in free union with all of the beneficent forces at work in the universe.

Of course, this experience, which can be had by a sincere disciple, and which I have just described briefly, may seem strange to some people; but thousands of people around the world have had such experiences—which, therefore, are not unknown to humanity. Moreover, every experience that a man has is worthy of respect and must be taken into account—whatever it may be.

Love rejects no being and considers no one as insignificant.

The Energy Of Evil Is All The More Dangerous When It Is Invisible

The question that you may be asking yourself now is:
Which source am I connected to?

From which fountain do I draw the water of my life?

For which energy am I the transmitter-receiver?

Be courageous in your experimentation; and tell yourself that evil, lies and ignorance are all the more dangerous when they are invisible.

There is no harm in being an unconscious servant of the negative; what is harmful is to remain one—to do nothing to change.

On earth, evil is everywhere, so it is impossible to avoid being visited by negative images and thoughts; but you must be conscious of them, and work internally to become the transmitter-receiver of the source of good and its alliance of light. You must unite yourself, in purity, with the currents of beneficent life, and strengthen them on the earth.

Only in this way will peace triumph.

May those who commit themselves to this path of unselfish service for the Supreme Good be blessed for all eternity.

No Act Is Insignificant

From now on, awaken to the fact that nature is alive, intelligent, and filled with influences. Therefore, you must respect it, and respect all of the beings which compose it—both the pleasant and the unpleasant ones.

Everything is worthy of respect because, behind every thing and every being, there is always Him—the single creator of the Whole.

Through nature and its inhabitants, it is always the divine spirit that you are meeting and looking for, because it is this spirit's love which gives life and evolution to all beings.

Through both the positive and the negative, a lesson is always being transmitted to you, so that you can become stronger and stronger, and raise yourself up higher—towards fullness.

If you make this thought come alive, by concentrating on it and by making it a part of you, then you will discover the kingdom of peace.

Nutrition, respiration, thoughts, words, gestures, feelings, desires—all of these constitute exchanges with the visible and invisible universe, and are not without consequence.

No action—as minute as it might be—remains without consequence, because nothing is cut-off from the Whole. Behind the tiniest bit of negativity stands the great reservoir of evil—just as, behind the tiniest bit of unselfish goodness, there stands the School of St. John.

Nothing is separated; everything is tied together.

Learn how to accomplish the tiniest bit of good dictated to you by your pure heart, and you will find the path that leads to us.

Human beings refuse to see this reality in front of them because they do not want to make any efforts to transform themselves, or to become responsible for themselves, their thoughts, their feelings, their life, their actions, and their involvement in the Whole.

What delights a disciple drives an ordinary man to despair.

The disciple rejoices in the idea that everything is tied together, because he sees in it the great means, the great method, for taking action in the world and spreading the light. The other man feels sorry for himself, because he feels like he is tied-up and thinks he can't do what he wants to do anymore—that is, live just any way, do just anything, be an unconscious servant of evil without being responsible for anything. This is the consequence of modern education. It is this deplorable mentality which is allowing the negative to triumph everywhere at the present time. A disciple does not deny the shadowy part that he carries within himself; instead, he consciously unites himself with the great force of good, and it is through this force that he finds the secret for transforming negativity, for controlling it, and for making it serve what is good.

No One Else Can Be Conscious For You

The teaching that I am proposing to you pushes you to become conscious, responsible, and the master of yourself. This is the sign of the School of Light. The other school pushes you to be unconscious and irresponsible, and to have no control over yourself.

The teaching is not for the unconscious, because, for them, there is no choice; they have given up their human nature and have sold their souls. If you can approach the teaching, it is because you are conscious. The more you increase this consciousness, with inner honesty, the more you will understand and have a choice.

Choice is always tied to consciousness and freedom. No one else can be conscious for you. If that happens, then you lose your being and your freedom.

When you are faced with a choice, you must wield the sword of decisions. This choice and this decision are valid for everything, because that is what it means to be conscious of exchanges—to be conscious and to have a choice in everything. Through every exchange, you can tie yourself to death or to life, to health or to illness, to peace or to war—the false peace.

Man himself is the key that opens up the doors to the universe—either the door to hell, or the door to heaven.

If you unite yourself with hell, you become its agent and you transform your environment into hell. It is the same for heaven.

This is where these words come from: *"You recognize a tree by its fruit."*

The tree of eternal life.

The tree of good mixed with evil, of life mixed with death.

Look at how humanity has transformed life on earth and you will know what it has tied itself to.

Those who reply that there is no other path are slaves who do not know what choice is, because they have sold their souls for a plate of beans.

They proclaim themselves to be the most intelligent and the most evolved people in the world—and they sell their eternal souls for a plate of beans.

What a magnificent sign of intelligence!

Without Purity, Peace Is Impossible

These days, everything is polluted, in every domain—physical, moral, mental, spiritual. Pollution is the sign of a distortion of the law of healthy evolution. It is an illness, an impurity, a non-respect for beings, a path of death.

The path of peace is found through a new awareness and a fundamental reversal. No one else can obtain this awareness and this reversal for you; it is, above all, individual and free. The person who commits himself to this path can become a pioneer in a new world—in a new, resurrected humanity. By his example, he will influence his entourage and encourage the whole world to commit itself to a new life.

Man has polluted the earth with pesticides, chemicals, nuclear radiation, etc.

He has polluted his own body with anarchical habits and industrialized foods—and in contradiction with the holy law of the cosmic intelligence.

He has polluted his life, and has lost his health, his immune system, his sleep, etc. He has polluted his desires through the development of the society of consumption, which turns him into a consumer. All of society is based upon this concept of the man-consumer. Without it, the present economic system would collapse. This is why the individual is transformed into a consumer by many different means—educational, hypnotic, magical, etc.; and this starts when he is still in his mother's womb.

Humanity has polluted its will and its personality by cutting itself off from the source of the spirit and by prostituting its eternal being to acquire material "goods" that are illusory and ephemeral. Material "goods" are not negative, but they must not be placed above everything else.

Humanity has polluted its heart, its thoughts and its spiritual soul by introducing lies, selfishness and dishonesty everywhere.

Music, philosophy, spiritual paths, culture, art, literature, love—everything is polluted.

If you reflect on these points and you understand—beyond the words—the message being sent out to you here, then you must turn away from all of that in spirit, and, on your own, create new bonds of light with nature and with your environment.

You must raise your thoughts up towards the Most High, in order to find the source of purity and to unite yourself with it.

Only the source of the spirit can purify the world. Without purity, peace is impossible.

Choose healthy, vegetarian foods. Eating meat is one of the greatest causes of war in the world, because the blood of all of those animals who are tortured and killed calls out for the blood of human beings.

Learn to respect life, and be filled with gratitude.

Open yourself up completely to the living nature and to its laws, with total simplicity and honesty.

Open your heart to love, your will to the force of good, and your thoughts to the cosmic wisdom.

Turn towards all that is truly pure, authentic, good, alive, sacred, noble, and great; and consciously unite yourself with the source of the Whole.

Cut the ties that unite you to the bad habits which lead to illness, death and war.

Turn away from the negative influences of the enemies of humanity and life. Refuse to practice their mysteries or to participate in their work of destruction.

The person who proclaims himself to be against war, yet never stops giving his life and his personality to the artisans of war, is a liar, if he's conscious, or one of the living-dead, if he's unconscious. We must not accept this dangerous situation into which humanity is plunging itself; we must not agree to become agents of evil—but awaken, fight, and unite ourselves with all of the beneficent forces at work.

These forces of Good exist; and the current of the humanity of St. John is the living proof of this.

The Truth Is Inside Of You

If you understand the key that we are offering you, then no force can prevent you from becoming a beneficent being—working for free peace and for the good of all beings, within the will of the Most High.

Every thought, feeling, word and action is a powerful, magical means for uniting yourself with the Source of good, the School of light, for attracting it inside yourself, and for spreading it all around you.

If you use this power of your personality to distance yourself from Good and from consciousness, then you will become a negative being.

The problem stems from the fact that every person in the entire world wants to make his own limited point of view triumph, and wants other people to see him as a champion of goodness and peace—whereas, in reality, he is a servant of evil and destruction, as a result of his inner life. The world is filled with lies. This is why I say to you: the truth is inside of you. It is by uniting yourself with the Source of Good that you will see it—right there, where it is—and no one will be able to deceive you ever again.

Everything Is Magical

Know that nothing in the world is without effect. Everything is magical; everything has an influence. If you are not conscious of this law, you will allow poisons to enter you—without knowing it. By always uniting himself with the negative, man ends up forgetting that there is a sublime world in which he can find nourishment and peace.

Today, only the devil arouses interest; only he sells. Human beings are greedy for blood, murder, noise and thrills.

But an initiate knows the origin, the meaning and the purpose of the smallest things. He knows that true mastery and force are not to be found in the lower, coarser side of life, but in subtlety and finesse; therefore, he strives to re-establish the balance between his body, the earth, his life, his desires, his person, his heart, his thoughts, and the pure spirit. In this way, he leaves the lower side, in order to elevate himself towards the revelation of the splendor of the spirit.

The great secret for establishing living and conscious exchanges with beings and things resides in love-wisdom. If you love something with force and intensity, then this love creates a bond which unites you to that thing. And this thing takes on a new dimension in your eyes.

If you direct your burning love towards the primordial source of every thing, while desiring to put yourself at its service, then a mystical force will open up inside of you and you will consider the world in a new way.

In everything, look for the path of love—the path that can enrich you, rejuvenate you, awaken you to life, make you better, and lead you towards fullness.

You are constantly performing exchanges with the living nature—with the earth, water, air, fire—so become aware, and let them help you to raise yourself up towards the spirit of light.

Every exchange that does not awaken your inner life weakens you and leads you towards death. Be alive; awaken. Be in love with the Whole; and, without further delay, put yourself at the service of the always-pure source of the spirit.

THE KINGDOM OF PEACE IS LIKE A WOMAN

The kingdom of peace is like an ordinary woman who loves life, her husband and her children, but who is always preoccupied by the many questions which create doubts and fears inside her soul.

Doubts and fears about life, her husband and her children—to such an extent that she ends up living in a state of anguish and irritation, with a hardened heart and hurtful words.

On a day when she is feeling very sad, with a circle of questions whirling around in her head, she mechanically approaches a stream out in nature, sits down near it, and listens to its soft music. This music, through some mysterious power, moves her consciousness into her heart, opens it, and begins to talk to her and to give her all the answers.

Filled with joy, she raises her eyes and, for the first time, sees the sparkling sun, the green grass, the majestic trees; everything speaks to her of love and joy, and invites her to fullness.

In truth, I say to you, the person who lives on the surface of life can only find suffering and become a carrier of war. The external man always lives with questions, fear and unhappiness; but the inner man, who lives inside the heart, knows all the answers. Not ready-made answers which generate new questions, but living answers which lead to fullness and peace.

Only truth brings the fullness of life, and freedom.

The source of the truth lives inside your heart; and if you let its waters flow, you will find the purity of your true being and you will know peace. Fear, doubt, anguish and irritation are impurities which prevent the waters of the heart from flowing, and the true love from manifesting itself. Let your heart open up and let the waters of your heart flow; and all of the impurities will flee far away from you.

The external man cannot find the peace that he needs so much if he is cut-off from the inner man, from the heart. The inner man cannot find the fullness that he needs so much if he is cut-off from the source of the true being.

Therefore, each one is dependent upon the other; the angel of peace needs man in order to achieve peace on earth, and man needs the angel of peace in order to bring his life to fullness.

I AM GENTLE AND HUMBLE OF HEART

If you aspire to peace, open up the door of great calmness inside your soul.

Calmness is a state of rest where everything is tranquil. Through calmness, find and cultivate the vibration of true gentleness.

Gentleness leads you towards the subtle world and allows you to manifest the superior love.

From gentleness, raise yourself up towards authentic humility—the one which puts you in your proper place, and opens up to you the path to the summit of the mountain of wisdom. Humility recognizes that there exists a reality which goes beyond everything, and allows you to discover the energy that you need to propel yourself towards it. From true humility comes the light of intelligence.

The key to humility is thankfulness. Learn to be thankful for everything—for what is good, and for the hardship which makes you grow. For the extraordinary, and for the ordinary.

The man who has no respect and no gratitude cannot climb the mountain of higher knowledge.

From humility, cultivate the patience and find the serenity of the person who acts in accordance with the holy law, and who is, therefore, on the path of victory.

Success comes to the person who knows how to desire in cosmic unison—and, then, how to wait.

Inside patience is hidden the great secret of realization. Indeed, man wants many things; but, in the end, it is always the divine that accomplishes and finishes the work begun.

From such a conception of life can come a great force and a profound serenity.

Patience is not a lack of interest, but the certainty that one is doing all that is necessary for success and that the final decision always belongs to the Most High.

The patience which results from calmness, gentleness and humility is similar to a state of superior consciousness, to the cup of profound silence, to a tranquility and an attentive immobility, through which the light of the revelation-truth, and of the peace which is not of the world, can come and manifest itself.

This sacred patience can only be obtained by working on oneself, through the practice of meditation and of spiritual discipline. You begin with tranquility and external immobility, then with an inner calm. This calm is deepened by gentleness and humility, until one attains profound silence through serene patience.

Become aware that calmness is, above all, a vibration, which you must cultivate in order to learn how to plunge yourself into it whenever you want to and in any situation. No one must be able to make you lose your calm, unless you yourself have decided to. This involves a long apprenticeship, which you will have successfully completed when you are capable of calming a stormy situation just by your presence.

Then, do the same thing for the vibration of gentleness—gentleness in your gestures, your feelings, your thoughts, your words, etc. Finally, for humility and patience. This is when serenity will appear; and, through it, you will get a taste of the great calmness of the spirit which is infinite and eternal.

You find yourself on the threshold of the world of the great souls.

This calmness of the spirit will always remain inside you as a point of superior consciousness, even in the middle of the worst agitations of the world. It will permanently remind you of the sublime reality of the superior world, which remains unchanged above the ephemeral illusions. Nothing can ever again disturb such a calm; and this is why the disciple is patient—because he is sure of the final victory. It is no longer he who aspires to find peace; instead, it is the peace of the kingdom that pursues him and calls out to him continuously.

Deep down, human beings do not know what peace is; they confuse it with tranquility or calmness.

Tranquility is easy to achieve; all one has to do is to eliminate all of the causes of external agitation. Calmness can only be internal, and it is, therefore, much more difficult to achieve. No man can run away from himself; and it is up to each person to face up to his own internal agitation.

Many people have tried with all their strength to establish this inner silence—but have not succeeded. The secret of the irresistible force is hidden inside patience. Strength comes from on-high, from eternity. Only the person who has reached eternity is strong, serene and patient. He is in harmony with the Whole. He knows—he sees—that everything is already accomplished "on-high" and that the rest must inevitably follow. Despair and doubts no longer have any hold over him.

Eternity is the tree of life, the kingdom of peace.

The cross of space and time is the tree of death. Life encompasses the ensemble, and death touches only pieces.

As soon as a piece is cut off from the ensemble, it loses its peace and disappears. If your hand is separated from your body, it dies.

The organs are the pieces and the body the ensemble. The pieces must work for the Whole and be attached to it.

If you yourself are separated from the Whole, from eternity, your life loses its meaning, and you are plunged into the kingdom of death—separated from calmness, gentleness, humility, or self-knowledge, and serene patience.

True peace is a force and a superior creativity; when it descends into the manifested worlds, it leads them onto the path of regeneration and evolution.

Be gentle and humble of heart, and you will find the true force of the I-Am spirit.

THE THREE KEYS

Wisdom, love and truth are three keys for achieving the kingdom of peace.

Wisdom is a food for man and the external world.

Love is a food for the inner man and the heart.

Truth is the foundation of life and unites one with the Eternal.

Without wisdom, man is plunged into the darkness of scholarly-ignorance and of mental deterioration.

Without love, he can only become selfish and nasty.

Without truth, he is lost inside the illusions of his own lies, and he sinks into unawareness of his authentic being.

Is this kind of man something to be desired?

Can he govern the world in peace?

Then, why is nothing done to educate human beings in this sense, and why is there no one to talk about these three virtues?

A spiritual student of the current of St. John must fervently strive to acquire these three virtues.

The truth is what he is here and now.

Love is the supreme force—the only thing that can protect him on the path and guide him towards the great Sun-Truth.

Wisdom is a light which comes out of him to offer peace to the external world as he is walking on the path of truth and love.

VEGETARIANISM FOR PEACE

If you aspire to become a servant of peace—both internal and external—and, therefore, of the humanity of light, then begin to think about vegetarianism.

I do not intend to give a lengthy explanation on this subject, because there are many books which deal with it. I am simply pointing out an orientation for the work in favor of the kingdom of peace—one which has always been followed, throughout the centuries, by the School of Life and Spirit.

Happiness and joy do not reside in the unconscious satisfaction of all of the suggestions proposed by the world—far from it.

The world invites you to drink and to eat just anything, to satisfy your palate and your stomach, to become rich and powerful at any price, to experience all sorts of sensations—like luxury, desire, idleness, etc. But, in reality, everything must be paid for; and, so, man loses his peace, his soul and his intelligence.

Happiness and joy reside in discipline and in conformity to the celestial order. The moment a man loses his free inner peace, he loses himself, and he becomes weak and easily influenced; he has no conscience, and he threatens, at every moment, to do evil, and to become its slave, its servant. Countless are those who, deep within their consciousness, recognize that they do not control their own lives, but that evil dominates them and is leading them—in spite of themselves—towards their fatal downfall. They have tied themselves to it, and now they think that they can no longer turn this situation around. In reality, man can always turn things around—because the door is always open, the hand always held out, and the force always present inside of him; all he has to do is make the decision and call upon it.

We are surrounded by good and bad influences, and it is up to us to choose which ones we want to be tied to. We must not let other people, or old habits, decide for us what kind of life we want to live. Being carnivorous has always been a sign of negative forces and of a profound degeneration in humanity.

By ingesting meat, man is nourishing himself in the kingdom of death. Medical doctors and scientists have finally acknowledged that the vegetarian diet—when it is well-balanced—is the best diet of all. So why hesitate?

The violence which pushes man to spill the blood of animals all over the earth is the same as the one which pushes individuals to kill each other. The blood thus spilled feeds legions of dark and negative spirits, which then enter human beings and push them towards war. Being carnivorous has, throughout time, been recommended and taught by the fraternity of darkness; and it is one of the principal causes of war, of illness, and of the non-mastery of oneself.

By becoming a vegetarian, you will be healed of many chronic illnesses, and you will avoid many others. You will be in harmony with the sacred teaching and the universal law of love and purity. You will feel more calm, and more the master of your own thoughts, feelings and desires.

Your life will be intensified; you will be less tired, and have much more strength and energy when exerting yourself.

Your nervous system will be strengthened, and you will become more receptive to the impressions coming from the invisible world.

Your inner life will become clearer, and you will feel a dignity, and a harmony with your deepest consciouness.

On the level of the worldwide service for peace:

- You will cut your ties with the negative influences, and will no longer give them any of your strength.

- You will purify the atmosphere of the earth.

- You will feel that you are working towards the pacification of every person's consciousness, in a natural and permanent way.

You will give strength to our Christly School and to our ideals of light—as well as to the egregor of the dove.

Understand that one can certainly work for peace if one eats meat, or that one can be a carrier of war even if one is a vegetarian. The initiatic teaching rejects no one; I am simply pointing out a very powerful method, based upon a deep and superior knowledge, which is addressed only to those who are ready to understand it in its true sense.

Happiness and peace are the product of effort—and not of a careless, casual attitude.

WORDS FOR AWAKENED MEN

All religions and all political ideologies preach: "Help the poor."

Christ said: *"The poor you will always have with you, but I will be here only for a short time."*

Yes, today the poor are Christ and his teaching, and the angel of peace, of wisdom and of love. They are starving to death, and they have no place to sleep or rest; and no one pays any attention to them, no one opens up their heart and their thoughts to them.

It is easier to give money than to invite the light and the pure teaching of Christ inside oneself. The only means for eliminating poverty lies in this welcome and this compassion directed towards the angels, towards luminous thoughts, and towards feelings that are noble, beautiful and true.

Just because we can't see them, that doesn't mean that thoughts and ideas don't exist. In reality, thoughts and ideas are living and independent beings which direct the world. There is a thought, a pure idea, of peace—just as there is one for Christ.

Everyone wants peace, but the angel of peace has never been so miserable.

Compassion, hospitality and charity for the angel of peace and the teaching of Christ.

THE HEROIC PATH OF SHAMBALLA

History Is Always Repeating Itself

The history of humanity reveals a great struggle for perfection and evolution.

The cosmic intelligence uses war to awaken human beings; and they all respond to its cyclical call.

On earth, man is required to choose between being a warrior, a knight, for the cause of darkness and destruction, or for that of the light and of harmonious evolution.

As a pilgrim for peace, embrace the cause of the light, and put yourself at the service of the will of the Supreme Good.

Those who do not know the will of the Sublime wander through the darkness of the ignorance of the goals of the universe. They are like the people who were having fun or going about their petty business while Noah was constructing his ark.

Just as they were two thousand years ago, Christ and his School are present and are working on earth. And what about you—what are you doing, and what is your relationship with him?

History is always repeating itself; what was before is now, and will be again, under different forms and to varying degrees.

History carries a message of wisdom within itself. It is not static; it is moving. It is pursuing a mysterious objective; it is leading humanity towards a precise goal which is visible only to those who have a pure heart and who are, therefore, able to succeed in elevating their consciousness all the way up to their soul. Only the soul knows the invisible golden thread onto which are grafted the images and events of history.

When Noah was building his ark, when Hermes Trismegiste was destroying the instruments of his science so that they would not fall into impious hands, and when Jesus accepted to drink the bitter cup and to be handed over to the Sanhedrin, they all knew the invisible plot of history and were consciously participating in the healthy evolution of humanity. The artisan of peace has no other choice but to consciously participate in the history and the harmonious development of the earth and of beings. Why do human beings live history passively, without taking part in it?

Only the person who has united himself with, and has contemplated, the goals of the universe can take part in history in a beneficial way

Entire civilizations have disappeared in cataclysms and in devastating wars—quite simply because they were no longer playing a role in history. They had reached a summit and had contributed their stone to the building, but, after that, they did nothing more; they were stagnating and were, therefore, holding back evolution. Thus, the kings and the leaders of peoples and nations too often believe that the destiny of their country or of the world is in their hands; but if they are not united with the cosmic intelligence, then this is an illusion.

Put The Will Of The Most High Above Everything Else

All of these civilizations and all of these great kings and leaders disappeared because they did not understand that they were supposed to be at the service of the luminous evolution, and that, above their own royalty and power, there was a higher power and royalty.

The Master teaches this truth to Pilate when the Roman says to him: *"I have the power to release you or to have you crucified."* He answers: *"You would have no power over me, had it not been given to you from above; that is why the one who handed me over to you is guilty of the greater sin."*

In that scene, we are witnessing the agony of a civilization which, having reached its summit, refuses to open itself up to the new, and chooses the path of destruction. It fights against the projects of the cosmic intelligence and condemns itself to evolution through suffering. What holds true for the history of humanity also holds true for us.

In every person, there is a Pilate and a Christ, an accuser and a representative of the old guard who does not want to change or adapt. All wars come from the fact that people are trying desperately to defend something which is destined to disappear anyway. Having turned away from the light emanating from the cosmic intelligence, humanity has placed itself naturally under the influence of the princes of destruction. Thus, everything that human beings build is destined to be destroyed. If you want to become an artisan of peace, you must work for what is eternal; you must become a warrior of love and wisdom.

To want peace in this world is to be a warrior in the service of Christ. The teaching of the initiates is the only one which can allow peace to triumph, because it is eternal; and it is eternal because it is united with the will of the Most High. It is not limited by the petty viewpoints of human beings—or by ephemeral things, or illusions, or considerations of race, of peoples, of boundaries, of nationality, of family, etc. The teaching of the humanity of light is universal; it is the source, the purity and the final goal of all of the religions, teachings and peoples of the earth. Nothing is foreign to it because it is one with the Source of the being.

The Idea Of A Humanity Of Light

Now here is the great secret of peace upon which you must meditate if you want to unite your spirit with the great spirit which embraces everything.

It is war and destruction which move history forward, since human beings refuse to obey the cosmic intelligence and are prisoners of the lying influences of the princes of destruction. They prefer lies, instead of the truth. War is not negative in itself, but it must be controlled, humanized and internalized; its goal must no longer be destruction, but harmonious construction in cosmic unison.

The individual man must become universal and live for the Whole.

If you look at the history of humanity in a new way, you will be able to see that, throughout the centuries, there has always been—hovering above the time—the idea of a humanity of light, living in peace and freedom, and also the idea of a land of light.

This idea is at the origin of every civilization and of every discovery; and it has revealed itself to be at the origin of all peoples. It has been like a guide, a motor, a hope, a sense for humanity. For some people, it has transformed itself into a vision giving real form to the supreme goal of all aspirations—happiness, peace, fullness, the lost paradise.

Every time that the sun of this idea has shone openly, humanity has known joy; but, as soon as they moved away from it, they were plunged into the darkness of tribulation and were deprived of peace—no longer able to succeed in attaining their true being.

The teaching of the initiates comes from this idea, and to enter the current of the man-John is to succeed in uniting oneself with this idea of light. Then the disciple understands the full value of this idea, and that his task—like that of all human beings—is to be its incarnation on earth, through his own personality, so that the humanity of the earth can also become a humanity of light, and so that the earth will be transformed into a sun and will become a pure chalice for Christ.

The Land Of Light Of The Guides Of Humanity

If, as a disciple of the humanity of light, you concentrate on this idea which shines in eternity, you will discover the sacred land which all of the legends have spoken of: the kingdom of Christ, the land of the living, the Terra Lucida, the celestial Jerusalem, the kingdom of Melchizedek, Shamballa. There live the Masters and authentic guides of humanity, the priests and kings in the order of Melchizedek—to which Jesus belonged.

All of the great Masters, the saviors and the healers of humanity have come with the vibration of this idea of light, and with the support of this holy land, in order to guide and awaken human beings upon the right path of life. Not to establish dead religions or systems of belief, but to educate humanity, and to elevate it in liberty towards the light of the spirit and the ultimate fulfillment.

Above the earth of low, coarse vibrations, and above the ignorant, selfish and proud humanity, shine a land of light where everything is pure and clear, a humanity with a pure and vibrant soul, and a sublime idea of happiness and perfection.

All beings are trying to find this idea, but they don't know it.

Raise your eyes up towards it, and you will become a servant of peace, a disciple of Christ, and a benefactor of humanity.

The Consecration To The Archangel Michael

From this sun of Shamballa emanates a luminous vibration which comes down onto the earth, through the divine teaching, in order to help the disciples. This vibration, which strikes down the dragon of lies, is called, in the tradition of esoteric Christianity, St. Michael. He is the guardian of the original image of the good man and is the guarantor of peace. He gives strength to those who aspire to serve Christ.

Of course, everything that I am saying here is esoteric, and can only be approached through reflection, meditation and the internal experience.

Go to a calm and tranquil place where you will not be disturbed.

Get into a comfortable position, keeping your back very straight.

Your body has been pacified beforehand:

– with food that is pure and vegetarian;

– with an ablution of water on your hands, face and feet;

– with clean clothes—either white or some other light color.

If you have done all of this, your meditation will be much more powerful. The more effort you put into something, the greater the results you will obtain.

Your body is calm and relaxed.

Breathe deeply and very gently three times from your abdomenal area; then let your breathing become natural.

Consciously think: "I am entering the kingdom of inner silence. Through this silence, I am present and conscious; I am awakening."

Now raise your thoughts and your internal vision upwards until you are contemplating the idea of the humanity of light, living in peace and freedom.

This idea contains all human dreams and aspirations.

Contemplate this idea, and maintain your concentration without falling asleep, or letting yourself be distracted or disturbed.

Be aware that you will have to overcome the trials and obstacles which are sure to put themselves between you and the idea. This is a battle, and you will need love and self-confidence to triumph.

The more you succeed in contemplating this idea in purity, the more you will perceive that you are moving closer to the reality of your own inner Christ-like consciousness—of your true being.

Then an internal knowledge about "man" can be naturally transmitted to you.

If you continue your concentration, the idea will take the form of a point of light around which one all of creation revolves. In this way, you will find your own center.

The second stage of the exercise consists of approaching the point of the idea until you succeed in entering it by means of your thoughts. This is when the land of light, the kingdom of God, and perfection will appear.

In the third stage, imagine a light flowing from Shamballa towards the physical earth and humanity in the form of the Archangel Michael—holding the sword and the scale. This light is like the light of the sun in its beneficial aspect; it brings wisdom for the mind, love for the heart, and strength for the will.

Look at how certain awakened human beings capture this presence of the solar archangel and become his servants on earth. They form his body—in a way—inside humanity.

Through the fourth stage of the exercise, consecrate yourself to the Archangel Michael; call his vibration down upon yourself and, through it, the vibration of the land and of the humanity of light.

> "Archangel Michael, guardian of unity and peace,
> I call upon you.
> Make me the servant of universal Good
> and strike down all of the darkness inside of me,
> so that I may be resurrected inside the light of the true being
> that I-Am eternally.
> In my earthly reality,
> I want to become a pure chalice for Christ.
> Let what flows from me with purity, beauty and creative force
> be sent out like a ray of light,
> and let it be spread, in union with you,
> like a luminous cloud over humanity.
> Amen."

Through this consecration, you make the commitment to become an artisan of peace, in the service of the idea of light which leads humanity through the centuries.

Then you must work in the secrecy of your heart for the good of all beings and for the triumph of the free peace of Shamballa and of the current of St. John.

Humanity In The Clutches Of The Dragon

The Archangel Michael wants to strike down the dragon—not to destroy it, but to put it in its place and subdue it. The dragon represents the force of lies and illusion which has invaded the human soul. The archangel's battle takes place in humanity through the heart and the consciousness of man—who is the unconscious prisoner of this dragon of ignorance. The fact that he can no longer see the land of light and that he cannot manage to find peace, either internal or external, is proof of this.

When a man has become aware of the grasp which the influence of the dragon of the personality has upon him, he strives to raise his eyes upwards and, in doing so, he liberates the sphere of his head. His thoughts are no longer in the clutches of instinct, and he is able to contemplate the land of light. Then he liberates his heart, and then his will; and this is when he is able to act in a new way in the world and to build the kingdom of the peace which does not come from this world. He becomes a servant of the Archangel Michael.

Of course, the human beings who are "so evolved" will never be willing to accept they are caught in the clutches of a negative force, which is dominating them and leading them towards slavery. This force is not negative in itself, because everything within nature is good—and it is this force which has created the human personality. But it becomes negative because it does not want the personality to evolve any more; it wants to monopolize it. Thus, human beings who believe themselves to be free and independent cannot, in reality, think, feel or act outside of their small and limited personality. This is what causes suffering.

The Art Of The Fight Which Saves

Faced with this kind of slavery, the awakened man can only revolt and put all of his strength to work in order to free himself. This is when he moves into the art of the fight which saves. When an illness enters his body, man has to fight it with all of his strength and by the use of intelligent means.

Thus, there exists an art of combat which has been transmitted throughout the centuries under the patronage of the Archangel Michael. The Knights of the Round Table and the Knights Templar were the most illustrious representatives of this sacred tradition in western civilization. This art is based upon a certain knowledge of good, upon the dignity of man, and upon the virtues of valor, ardor, idealism, mysticism and courage.

The knight fights, above all else, against himself, since the external world is nothing more than a reflection of man's internal world. Therefore, his first quality must be to not be afraid of himself.

The fear of death, the fear of what he is going to discover inside himself if he looks deep-down, the fear of not being equal to the task—these are the things that lock man up inside tiny boxes.

The person who wants to live for the good of the Whole has to have conquered his fears in order to be able to stand upon firm ground. There is no stability in fear—no security and no peace. The person who thinks that it is the work of others to build peace gives up his being because he is afraid. Being afraid is not negative; but the world is inhabited by cowards who present themselves as heroes.

The truly heroic path is silent and goes unnoticed in this world. It is within the reach of every person and is not reserved for an elite group. The heroic path belongs to the person who seizes it.

To put oneself at the service of the idea of the land of light, of pure thoughts, of noble feelings and of just actions, by inviting them into oneself in silence—that is a heroic act. Performing this action not for oneself but to help Christ to triumph—that is something which is admirable. This is a powerful key for peace—to offer oneself, for ten minutes each day, as a chalice for pure and sacred thoughts, and to radiate them into humanity. These thoughts no longer have anywhere to go because no one wants them.

This is a sacred service which must be performed with total selflessness, freely, and without personal benefit; it must be done only for the sake of goodness and for the freedom of goodness.

These days, goodness is manipulated and monopolized by all of the different parties which want to make use of its aura in order to have their own ideas triumph and to destroy their enemies. As a result, goodness itself is polluted, and no one knows what it is anymore.

The School of St. John absolutely does not want to bring a new religion, ideology or philosophy into the world, but, instead, to lead each individual to freely experience the source of life and spirit. Every person who unites himself with the source can make it flow inside himself and into the world. That is the kingdom of fullness, of abundance and of love. Goodness lives inside the human soul, and it is inside your own soul that you must find it.

O you, inside whom the pure teaching fans the fire of your heart,
You who perceive the beauty of the world of the soul,
You will be the soldier and the builder of the new kingdom of peace.

THE KINGDOM OF PEACE IS LIKE PURE WATER

The kingdom of peace is like water that is pure, clear and perfectly calm—and upon which is reflected the immensity of the moving cosmos.

In truth, I say to you, make your life and your consciousness like this water, and you will find profound peace which will never leave you.

Peace is a cosmic harmony, a universal symphony, which—once it has entered the soul—can never leave it again.

The peace which one can lose is not the true peace, but only a stage.

THE EGREGOR OF THE DOVE AND THE TRIUMPH OF FREE PEACE

The Free And Creative Man

For those who truly aspire to work for peace, I pronounce these loving words.

Peace, harmony and order exist on their own in the cosmos. In reality, it is inside man that they are missing.

The cosmos is obliged to have peace as its foundation; otherwise, everything would disappear. Everything that it builds has the universal order as its foundation.

Man is made in the image of the cosmos, but there is a part of him which is free, and with which he can give birth to disharmony or to harmony.

Meditate deeply upon this truth:

The cosmos is a creator in the sense of a supreme will.

The human being in the image of the cosmos is a free creator; he can oppose order and beauty.

All of his thoughts, feelings, words and gestures—formed either consciously or unconsciously—are living beings which move about inside his respiratory atmosphere and have an influence upon him, upon his immediate entourage, and upon the world.

No man can help but be a creator inside the subtle world; and, therefore, he is responsible for what emanates from him.

Many people believe that they can live in just any way and think just anything, and that this will have no influence or repercussion on themselves or on their entourage; but that is an error, a false conception of life adopted by the person who refuses the responsibility of being an authentic man.

Man's strength can only come to him from his conscious union with the cosmic order. This is when he will become an artisan of peace. If he separates himself from this conscious union, he risks losing the meaning of life, beauty, peace and goodness; and then he will be able to give birth only to gargoyles and monsters.

Human beings have filled the earth's spiritual atmosphere with bloodthirsty monsters—and now they have to hide and protect themselves.

The person who turns away from the beneficent order can then do nothing else but serve the maleficent disorder. Until human beings understand the simplicity of reality and change their attitude, the climate of the world will continue to deteriorate. It's only logical—the person who sows a seed of peace and light in his field will harvest a fruit of peace and light, which he will share with everyone. The person who sows a seed of discord and darkness, or who allows the world to sow such a seed inside of him, will be obliged to live in war and pain.

You are constantly sowing seeds inside yourself through your thoughts, your feelings and your actions. You must be conscious of this, and strive to unite yourself with the highest thoughts, feelings and actions of the humanity of light, so that the future can be brighter.

Man plants the seed and it is the universe that makes it grow. This is the law. The person who breaks the law, by sowing ugliness and disorder in the garden of the Eternal, will suffer.

So choose a moment during the day when you can raise yourself up towards beauty, poetry and harmony. Look at your thoughts and your feelings, as if they were exposed in front of you in an art gallery, and strive to make them luminous, beautiful and celestial, in order to send them out into the world.

Concentrate on a beautiful thought or a noble feeling. Develop it and turn it into a veritable work of art by the means of your imagination.

Then expose this work before all of the beneficent spirits of the invisible world and offer it to the egregor of the dove.

No man should accept living in ugliness and baseness. All of the thoughts and feelings which degrade and demean the human condition must be left behind, as he elevates himself above them, into the kingdom of the sovereign spirit.

The more man agrees to descend into the dispossession of his worthy and noble being, the more he will lose his freedom. The more he elevates himself into the heights of the spirit, the more creative and free he becomes in cosmic unison.

No external condition can prevent an individual from raising himself up in spirit towards the kingdom of ideal beauty and of peace—so that he can then re-create them inside himself.

The Egregor Of The Dove: Source of The True Peace

Now, I am going to assume that we agree on the fact that every human being is potentially a free creator—through his thoughts, his feelings and his deliberate actions. But can he create anything all by himself? No. He always needs to unite himself with something. In order to create a child, the man needs to unite himself with a woman, and the woman with a man. This law applies to thoughts, feelings, and even actions.

It is because he consciously unites himself with the egregor of the dove, with St. John's humanity of light, with the cosmic order, with the Most High, that a disciple is able to become an artisan of peace, a son of God.

Without this internal union with the egregor of the dove, it is impossible to work for peace. Human beings accept the fact that it is not possible to create a child without the union of the two principles—masculine and feminine; but, when it comes to the laws of the spiritual world, they don't understand anything anymore.

Peace is a child which appears through man's union with the cosmic order.

The Art Of Creating Gods

Now, in order to clarify this point, I have to explain what an egregor is.

An egregor is a collective being composed of a multitude of influences which unite around a common center. For example, you are an egregor, because your body is composed of billions of cells which form your universe. Each cell is autonomous and has its own life; and you are like their global intelligence.

Humanity, too, is an egregor, because every individual who is part of it has a life which is more or less autonomous and free; but humanity is also a whole, with a global intelligence.

The egregor is always an invisible and spiritual being, which is coupled with a physical entity. When several people on the earth unite around a common idea, they give birth to an egregor—a collective and intelligent spiritual being; this being is then going to become independent and have its own life—which will be capable of influencing human beings and history.

This is a terrifying secret which was carefully hidden inside the ancient mysteries. They called it: "The art of creating Gods".

Then there was the war of the Gods; the egregors fought one another, and forced human beings to do the same. Man became a pawn in the hands of the egregors. He became the slave of the beings which he himself had created; and now he is obliged to feed them with his blood and his life.

Every political party, every group, every religion and every country has its egregor—with its forms, its influences, its orientations, and its specific intelligence.

Now, because man is capable of creating ugliness and of going against the cosmic order, he has generated negative egregors which push beings to kill one another—in spite of themselves—and to fight against evolution.

These negative egregors are eternal and independent; and only the humanity that has been initiated into the secrets of the light will be able to conquer and transform them.

There are also beneficent egregors, which are born out of man's union with the celestial order—and, more particularly, with the angelic world, which is the realm of purity.

Only the angelic world knows true purity.

The Thursday Ceremony Of The Students Of The School of St. John

If a group of human beings, aspiring to know peace in purity, come together inside a sacred atmosphere and turn their thoughts towards the angel of peace, they form a pure, luminous and beneficent egregor which rises up towards the Supreme and becomes a means of communication with the angel of peace.

Through this kind of emanation and creation, the human world and the angelic world can meet and form an alliance.

Such an egregor exists on the earth; it is the guardian of the true peace, and those who aspire to peace must make their luminous thoughts, their prayers and their meditations converge towards it.

This egregor of the dove was formed by the greatest initiates, at the cost of great sacrifice, and, in particular, by the Virgin Mary. It has been constantly maintained and vivified, throughout the ages, by the current of St. John; and it is once again the task of the School of Life and Spirit to accomplish this work for the good of all beings. The School of light accomplishes this task in different ways, and, in particular, by means of a ceremony for peace which is performed by some of its students every Thursday for 24 hours without interruption. It involves a relay and a circle of light for peace.

So, on Thursdays, you, too, can tie yourself internally to this work, through your thoughts, and contribute to the reinforcement of the egregor of the dove.

You can also perform this meditation on Thursdays in sympathetic communion with the work of the School of St. John.

– Wash your hands conscientiously, with the thought that you are going to perform a sacred act, an unselfish service for the good of all beings and for their healthy evolution.

– Go to a place that is conducive to reflection, and where you are sure that you will not be disturbed.

– Allow your body to enter a state of relaxation; at the same time, straighten yourself up, both internally and externally (spinal column). This straight position should not be tense but harmonious, and should correspond to an awakening of the body inside the presence of a soft light of the spirit.

Breathe deeply and very gently from the abdomen three times; then let your breathing become calm and regular. All of the worries and the agitation of the outside world leave you; you enter your sacred inner world.

– Let the silence surround you with this cloak; and feel your heart, in the center of your chest, becoming hot and opening up like a flower in the sun.

Your consciousness awakens inside your heart and communes with all that is best in you.

– Through your thoughts, raise yourself upwards, and imagine, above you, the beautiful blue of the sky in the mountains.

Consciously think:

"Above all people and every person, the unique light of the cosmic intelligence, which illuminates all of us.

Above all people and every person, one unique love which gives warmth to all of us.

Above all people and every person, one unique life which gives life to all of us."

– Then, in the blue of the sky, let a white dove appear.

– Let the cosmos think "peace", and let it form a pure thought of peace inside of you.

– Let this thought come down towards you until it penetrates the space occupied by your chest and your heart.

– Then feel this thought of peace very deeply.

– Let this pure and deeply-felt thought fill up your whole being.

– Bring this deeply-felt thought of peace to life. Let it become you, and you become it.

– Let this free peace live inside of you and deliver you from the hold of negative states of being and of all kinds of conditioning.

– Let the vibration of this peace which is not of the world reveal to you your true, profound, eternal being.

– The vibration of peace starts to become gentler and more subtle; it transforms itself into love, and into a soft, transparent, golden light which spreads all around you and envelops you.

– It keeps spreading until it surrounds the earth and envelops all peoples and all beings.

– You feel yourself inside this aura of the egregor of free peace.

– Internally pronounce these words—while thinking them, feeling them and living them in harmony with the angel of peace:

"May the light of the dove and the fire of the Holy Spirit transform all of the consuming fires of conflict into fires of creative work for the good of all beings and of the universe."

– Remain a few moments in silence. Open your eyes very slowly, and go back to your daily activities.

Know that, at the very moment when you are performing this sacred service each Thursday, you are not alone, because there are students of the School of St. John and of the humanity of light who are also working—and they are one with you.

Consciously unite yourself with them, and you will feel stronger, supported and helped.

If you perform this work, I thank you with all my heart.

Every human being should do this kind of meditation at least seven times during the year, even if it is only to give thanks for all of the blessings of life and to participate actively in the beneficent work of evolution.

This is a powerful way to illuminate and to transform one's future destiny.

The Mystery Of The Egregors

The sincere spiritual student must meditate deeply upon this idea of the egregors which unite human beings and the cosmic forces.

The egregors that are created unconsciously, and in fits of passion, live only to destroy, giving birth to instincts of power and domination inside their members. They are the true cause of war and of the conflicts pitting everyone against everyone else.

There are luminous egregors, created by the cosmos, which govern nature, minerals, plants, animals, human beings, the seasons, the planets, etc.

There are egregors for countries, for science, for justice, for politics, for the economy, for social life, etc.

The task of these egregors is to lead human beings onto the path of evolution; but, when their spiritual substance is polluted, they become sick, or even shrouded in darkness, and lead human beings to their downfall.

Originally, it was human beings who, in union with certain spiritual powers, generated the egregors of science, of medicine, and of Canada or any other country. But, then, they lost control of them; and these egregors directed them in such a way as to make them become unconscious and passive. As soon as an egregor causes blood to flow—in any manner whatsoever—it soils its inner light with an instinctive power and becomes a negative force of domination.

There are pure, celestial egregors—guardians of the sacred teaching of the humanity and the land of light.

The School of the humanity of St. John is the receptacle of all of the pure and sacred egregors of the good and worthy man. When we say "St. John", we do not mean just the Master—the beloved disciple of Christ—but a certain inner quality of the universal man, which this Master attained.

For example, when a man says the words "I am Canadian", he is saying this because he belongs to the egregor of Canada, and this egregor is speaking in him—and not the original, universal, eternal man living in the light of the truth.

The person who says "I am a citizen of the world" already has a broader vision of reality; he is already part of an egregor which is much larger, more peaceful and more awakened.

The person who says "I am a citizen of the infinite cosmos, and, inside myself, I carry all of the beings of the universe" is very close to the authentic being, the true man, the man-John. This enlarged conception of life absolutely does not prevent him from being Canadian, or anything else, but he won't be it unconsciously; and, with this attitude, he helps to heal the egregor of Canada.

The fundamental question which every disciple of the angel of peace must ask himself forcefully is this: "Which egregor do I belong to; which one do I feed and support with my commitment, my thoughts, my feelings and my actions?"

Often man believes that he is the one doing the thinking and desiring; he does not realize that he is dominated by an egregor, evoked unconsciously in the past. Therefore, it is of vital necessity to take back one's independence in the face of the enslaving collective powers, in order to unite oneself with the pure and sacred egregors which elevate man into the true light of the free being.

We live in a time when the invisible light which surrounds the planet and unites all beings to one another has been polluted.

Love, wisdom, honesty, goodness, justice, the consciousness of exchanges, friendship, etc.—all of these things must find a new purity again, so that humanity may once again find the true path of its harmonious evolution.

This is the work of the egregor of the dove and of the solar School of St. John.

Thank you for your precious help.

THE KINGDOM OF PEACE IS LIKE
A PERSON WHO IS WALKING

The kingdom of peace is like a person who is walking on a mountain path. Captivated by the beauty of the landscape, and discovering the infinite horizon before him, he stops and shouts his name out to the universe. Then the echo makes his voice reverberate seven times into distant worlds.

In truth, I say to you, the universe responds to every one of your manifestations. No power in the world can separate you or isolate you from the cosmos. You are in perpetual contact with it through all of the components of your being. If you are constantly shouting "I hate you", the universe will answer the same thing back to you.

If you say to it: "Everything for me, nothing for the others," it takes everything away from you, because everything comes from it.

If you go in the direction of "I love you", then the cosmos declares its love to you and offers you all of its treasures.

Other people will behave towards you in the same way that you have behaved towards them; know that you cannot lie to the invisible world, which sees everything and knows everything better than you do.

A simple thought or a tiny little wish coming from you can tie you to hell or to heaven.

No person can find peace without consciously uniting himself with the cosmic harmony, by cultivating inside himself the celestial thoughts, feelings and actions which will bring him into contact with the whole universe.

The universe rejects and imprisons those who cultivate disorder, unconsciousness and the great just-anything. All those who might disturb the cosmic order are kept away from the kingdom of free peace.

It is man who limits himself by his ignorance of the law of universal love.

The person who works in accordance with this key will get results; that is a certainty.

Instead of remaining inside negative states of being which feed the egregors of war, it is better to use your inner creative power to direct your thoughts, your heart and your will towards the positive realms, in order to tie yourself to the beneficent beings who are able to correct the situation and to transform life.

Through his unconscious negative thoughts, man is constantly tying himself to the darker spiritual realms, which attract unhappiness and pain to him and to the world; then he complains about his fate, which only makes things worse.

Peace and happiness belong to those who are ready to take their lives into their own hands, and not to blame others for their unhappiness.

If you are suffering, it is because your life, both internal and external, is not in harmony with the celestial order. The person who disturbs the celestial order, through his thoughts and his feelings, attracts the penalty of suffering to himself. Suffering is one of the forms of war.

The person who, making use of his freedom of consciousness and of life, decides to unite himself, through his thoughts, with all that is best, to forgive all of his enemies, and to love all beings in the image of the creator, attracts to himself, from the confines of space, indescribable influences of light and peace. Present-day humanity has cut itself off from the best, the beautiful, the true, and the sublime, which exist in the world of the spirit. Materialism and generalized baseness have killed the spirit of idealism and of cosmic union.

Friend upon the path of new life, do not let dark influences penetrate inside you and direct your destiny anymore; instead, from this moment on, unite yourself with what is the most celestial, divine, sacred, and positive.

"Look for the kingdom of heaven, and everything else will be given to you in addition."

THE TRUTH DOES NOT ASK YOUR OPINION

There is absolutely no possibility of establishing a lasting peace in the world if human beings do not become disciples of the Truth and of the universal teaching which flows from it.

The truth is—all on its own. It is eternal, always victorious. It has nothing to do with the limited opinion of human beings who quarrel over personal points of view. The person who moves away from the Sun-Truth is plunged into the darkness of ignorance and the abyss of suffering.

The truth is spread out everywhere; it is intelligent, sensitive and alive. It is the universal Word which is at the beginning of every thing and which is one with the source of God. Thus, it speaks to all beings, and it is all beings; it is speaking to you at this very moment, and, at this moment, you are truth.

You want to know the truth; look at yourself at this moment and you will know the truth. The truth is what you are in the present.

So all beings are truth; all beings are pure in the present, and they must all be taken into consideration.

The truth belongs to no one; it belongs to itself, and to those who have made themselves capable of receiving it.

Above all of the tiny opinions, there is the great truth, and it is towards this that you must elevate yourself.

Throughout all of the ages, there have been human beings who have succeeded in uniting themselves with the great truth and serving it with purity.

This universal Brotherhood-Sisterhood has left traces of its existence everywhere. It is the source of all of the good that has appeared in humanity and on the earth.

Human beings do not want to recognize the one truth because they have tied themselves to all kinds of impurities, negative things, prejudices, selfish interests, and habits which they do not want to give up; and this is why they prefer to make war.

Even you—if you do not adopt the teaching of the man-John, of the man who is united with and who serves the truth, then you will have no other choice but to become an agent of war.

These words do not come from a lack of tolerance or from a partisan attitude—quite the contrary; but they do reflect the reality. The truth is universal; it belongs to everyone and has no preference. It is man who must put himself at its service without bias, and not the truth that has to serve the personal and limited interests of one man—to the detriment of another.

Peace, truth, freedom, happiness, purity and self-knowledge are different words which describe one and the same reality.

Human beings think that they are going to build peace and live in happiness mechanically and artificially, without looking for the great truth, and while continuing to fight against the teaching of the humanity of light and of the inner man.

No peace is possible for the person who has not opened up his heart to the great force of universal good in purity, who has not united his thoughts to the wisdom of the worlds, and who has not attained the knowledge of his true, free and eternal being.

Without the authentic teaching of the initiates, no peace is possible within humanity; understand this, and get to work without delay. Peace is a state of superior consciousness which flows naturally from the source, and which—all by itself—re-establishes perfect order, harmony and justice with all of the elements of creation.

Try to find out who you are—not just inside your outer shells, but also in the superior and divine reality. Become a disciple of the free peace and the truth which reveal themselves inside of you within a state of superior consciousness, and you will find the secret paths which lead to our brotherhood of light.

THE KINGDOM OF PEACE IS LIKE
A FLOWING SPRING

The kingdom of peace is like a flowing spring. No matter what one pours into its water, it never stops flowing; it always remains pure and keeps its identity.

In truth, I say to you, purity—that is, being oneself, not mixed with anything else—is the origin of peace.

What upsets peace and harmony always comes from a foreign element, from an impurity which has been introduced into the body.

When a man is united with the source of the universal spirit, and the water flows through his soul, his intelligence, his thoughts, his heart, his will and his life, all the way into his heart, then he knows himself above and below, and no impurity can anchor itself inside of him; he is true, unmixed, pure, free, at peace and radiating peace. Everything around him becomes harmony.

The person who is in harmony produces harmony; the person who is in chaos generates chaos.

Concentrate on this idea of purity. Look for it and invite it into everything you do; and, one day, you will discover your true being and eternal peace.

There is no purity without discipline.

There is no discipline without a free inner awakening.

There is no awakening without an internal call from the soul.

There is no internal call from the soul without a superior reality.

There is no superior reality without the presence of the sovereign and invisible spirit.

Find who you are inside the source of the spirit and you will know purity and peace.

It is at the source of the spirit that the water of life is pure.

Without purity, there is no true self-knowledge, and, therefore, no mastery, no harmony, and no peace.

THURSDAY'S CIRCLE OF PEACE

If you could go up into space in order to contemplate our planet Earth from on-high, you would discover the beautiful blue planet of aerial photographs. But, opening up the eyes of your heart, you would soon perceive dark stains, crossed by lines of dark-red light, in the location of all of the large cities and capitals of the world. Before your astonished eyes, these spots of living energy would become larger and would finish by joining together to surround the earth and isolate it from the rest of the cosmos.

    This is the state of the earth from the spiritual point of view. Of course, there are, here and there, rays of pure color which emerge and pass through the dark cloud—like the Archangel Michael's sword piercing the dragon's body; but these remain very weak. This cloud is made up of all of the dishonest conceptions, the selfishness, and the low and unconscious thoughts, emotions and actions of human beings. The big cities have become immense cesspools and swamps, whose putrid odor spreads out over the whole earth.

Behind this dark cloud exists a pure land, a land of light and peace which completely surrounds the physical earth. All initiates and all disciples of the current of St. John and of its solar School are in harmony with this sacred land of luminous thoughts, of the heart filled with love, of the noble sentiment, of the just and unselfish act, of the pure and universal life.

If, for a few minutes, all human beings would put themselves, in unison, on the same wavelength as this land of light, if they would invite it inside themselves and radiate its vibration all around them, then the cloud of negativity could be dissolved and the blue sky of peace could appear once again.

This is one of the mystical goals of the circle for peace which is performed every Thursday by the students of the School of light. Every man and woman of good will can offer a few minutes of their time to unite themselves with this magical work, in order to bring about the triumph of peace and light on the earth.

Everyone can do it. It is not necessary to be a great intellectual or to have any diplomas; all one needs to do is to desire the good of all beings, with honesty, for a few minutes.

Humanity is an enormous battlefield! Who can think of resting while the battle is raging and the future of humanity is being decided with every new day?

Every Thursday, you have the chance to start doing something for peace, by uniting yourself—through your thoughts and your inner life—to an internal and concrete body of work.

May the angel of peace guide you upon the path of life.

THE KINGDOM OF PEACE IS LIKE A MOTHER

The kingdom of peace is like a mother who loves her child as a continuation of herself and who is capable of sacrificing herself for him. This is when she perceives that she carries all of humanity in her bosom, and that the whole of humanity is her child. Being the youngest, the child is closer to the divine; and it is he who becomes the master.

In truth, I say to you, the person who has never sacrificed himself for a higher good, who has never given something of himself for another person, does not know what love is.

Love always manifests itself in the new; it is the only thing that rejuvenates life and elevates it towards the Most High.

Behind the small love and the small sacrifice for a limited child hides the great universal and unlimited love. The person who has not found this love has not known love. The small selfish love must be sacrificed for the great love of the Whole. The person who does not make this sacrifice on his own will be forced into it by the world. All beings must sacrifice themselves in order to find the Most High. The law of sacrifice is the highest one taught by the living example of Christ.

The Masters of humanity teach by their living example.

Of course, sacrifice is frightening, but the person who has love knows that he is not going to lose anything; he is simply going to grow.

In order to accomplish the sacrifice of Christ, many incarnations of preparation are needed.

The Master St. John said: *"The person who says he loves God, but who does not love his Brother, is a liar."* It is possible to add to these words: *"The person who loves his Brother in the love of God and who does not put himself at the service of humanity, within the will of the Supreme Good, is a liar; he is just trying to give himself a clear conscience."*

The path of service is a preparation for the sacrifice of one's illusory being for the great reality. In this kind of sacrifice, the disciple of good loses nothing, because it is in sacrificing the lie that one finds the truth. Such a sacrifice is a transformation, an ennoblement and an elevation of the individual.

When all human beings are capable of transforming all negativity, through the virtue of sacrifice, with a view to the good of the whole, while being guided by wisdom, then the kingdom of peace will be possible.

THE ORIGIN OF WARS

When human beings have accumulated a lot of dark thoughts, negativity, unhappiness, crimes, lies, etc., war makes its appearance, in order to perform a large-scale cleaning operation, through the means of suffering and pain. The whole negative side receives the authorization of the Most High to break loose and to do whatever it wants.

Human beings really have to be blind and stupid not to realize that war is the work of the enemies of humanity. The ones who are the most conscious say: "War is unavoidable, because all of the accumulated negativity really must have a way of expressing itself; we cannot contain it indefinitely."

Right—no one can contain what is negative; and that is why it is necessary to avoid producing it—through a luminous education of humanity. By making the unconscious conscious, and through the art of spiritual alchemy, all negativity can be transformed into good. In God, there is no evil; and, when everything goes in the direction of God, evil does not exist anymore. Evil and disharmony come from a disorder, of which human beings are the cause. Eliminate this disorder and you will eliminate the cause.

When Christ came to bring the keys of light, humanity put him to death; and it continues to do so every day.

Human beings prefer to feed their inferior nature, to the detriment of the divine nature—and then they're surprised that they suffer.

Every injustice, every crime, every lie, every form of waste, and every violation of the cosmic order and of the teaching generates the causes of a future external war.

Refusing to admit the truth to themselves, human beings try to justify war and its abominations by means of a positive ideal.

But there is no justification whatsoever for revelling in baseness or for conspiring against the truth in the name of the so-called good of humanity.

The small selfish good must be put aside in favor of the universal good; only then does man triumph on every plane.

THE KINGDOM OF PEACE IS LIKE A CHEMIST

The kingdom of peace is like a chemist doing an experiment in his laboratory. He mixes the ingredients with great precision because he knows that, with the slightest error, his work will end in failure.

In truth, I say to you, thoughts, feelings and desires are like chemicals. Their mixture can result in a harmonious work, in an explosion, or in poisoning.

Some people ask that the power of thoughts and feelings be demonstrated to them—but is it necessary to prove the obvious? The person who no longer sees what is obvious has become so brain-dead that he will no longer see anything beyond his own self-importance.

If you want to know the chemical power of thoughts and feelings, look at the state of being you're in. If you live in harmony and self-control, then it means that your mixture and the elements chosen are correct. If you find yourself plunged into anguish, cacophony, ignorance, fear and weakness, then this means that the mixture is not good; you are being poisoned. If your internal fuses have blown out and you don't know where you are anymore, it means that you have produced an explosion inside yourself. Don't worry—everything can be put back into the right order; all you have to do is to clean up the laboratory a little and introduce new elements that are harmonious, pure and positive.

The person who does not know the nature of the elements that go into and come out of him—in the form of thoughts, feelings and desires—is running the risk of blowing up at any moment and of attracting all kinds of illness and misfortune to himself.

Being a man is like a cooking recipe: if the right ingredients are brought together and mixed with skill, the cake or the dish is a success. But if it's the great just-anything that is in command, then you can expect the worst—and the worst happens.

Become the master of your thoughts, your feelings and your actions; consecrate yourself to the service of the light of the spirit of good—and you will become a true man, a man-John.

THE WILL OF THE MOST HIGH

Meditate upon this idea; make it live inside of you until it agrees to open up its heart and to reveal its precious treasure to you.

Just like a human being, an idea has to be seduced, and made to feel confident, before it will open up its heart.

Everything that has been created by the cosmic intelligence is good. Absolute good exists, but not absolute evil—because, in every being, there is always a good side: the divine side. Evil comes from a disorder caused by creatures, and not by the creator. Thus, a good thing put in a bad place becomes negative. When every thing is put in its place, everything becomes good. This is purity—the original will of God, of the sublime love.

If a creature does not respect the good law of this will, then evil appears. "You yourself, as a creature—you are a good being; and, therefore, you must find your place in the will of the Most High. Then you will know your origin and your goal, your destiny. This kind of knowledge and its free fulfillment will give birth to peace and to the force of the good without shadows."

THE KINGDOM OF PEACE IS LIKE A GARDENER

The kingdom of peace is like a man cultivating his garden so that the people around him can enjoy the best fruits and vegetables.

In truth, I say to you, only the person who plants a seed will know its force. Plant the seed of good in your internal earth; experience it in your life, and you will discover the path of peace and of the eternity of the soul.

Unite yourself with the force of good, in humility and purity. Begin with the simplest and most insignificant act of goodness, and do it with total unselfishness.

For example, place the palm of your right hand over the rose of your heart, in the center of your chest. Perform this gesture gently and consciously, while thinking of the great love of Christ. Touch your heart and feel its warmth; then, in front of yourself, make a circular arc, parallel to the ground, with your hand (palm turned upwards)—while, at the same time, wishing all of the best to all beings.

You will notice that this act of goodness awakens your consciousness with even more clarity; it makes you stronger, and more the master of yourself.

Then perform this same exercise with a light of wisdom—that is, while awakening in the understanding of what you are doing.

Good must always be performed in harmony with the wisdom of the worlds.

If you invite inside yourself the seeds of good with wisdom, you will become stronger than all of the negativity in the world, and you will come to know the fruits of peace.

Peace is possible only when the inner man has become the master of the external conditions and conditionings.

The gardener who allows the seeds of the weeds which choke the good seeds to be planted in his ground is stupid.

The person who can no longer tell the good seed from the bad is totally lost. He urgently needs a good teacher.

Start by performing the smallest act of goodness with humility, and you will rapidly become capable of the greatest one. When universal good is the guide, even anger becomes positive, because it is channeled upwards.

It is not necessary to travel thousands of kilometers, to go all the way to Jupiter, or to spend years studying in universities, in order to find the force of good. It is present everywhere; it is right there where you are at this moment. It lives inside of you and all around you. All you have to do is call upon it, and it will come to you immediately. Perform an act of goodness, and you will start the flow of the source of your true being—which will purify you and reveal peace to you.

The task of every man who comes into this world is not just to learn how to read and write, to earn money, to have a family, and to experience all kinds of pleasure; it is also—and especially—to leave the darkness, in order to enter into the internal light which illuminates every man coming into this world. Everything else falls into second place.

The light of good, illuminating the inner life and leading it towards a state of higher consciousness, is a reality which every person can master; and, yet, no one teaches it in a practical way.

Cultivate unlimited goodness in your thoughts and in your heart, and offer the fruits of it all around you.

The force of good can manifest itself through a thought, a word, a feeling, a quality of the air, a desire, and a just action.

ABOUT THE AUTHOR

Olivier Manitara is a free spiritual teacher. Although he is self-taught, his work is part of an ancestral tradition of light. Born in France in 1964, he began, at a very young age, to instinctively practice exercises which would later prove to be spiritual in nature; he experienced his very first illumination at the age of 12.

At 19, he found himself at a turning point in his life and met a Master who gave a definitive direction to his work.

In 1987, after a period of following several teachings, he decided to go on a three-year retreat, part of which was spent in the mountains of Montsegur in the French Pyrenees. During this retreat, he developed a program of intensive activities in order to achieve his inner goal.

As a result of the intense experiences which he had undergone, he decided to devote himself entirely to the awakening of the human consciousness, and to freedom.

In 1991, he founded an initiatic School within the current of St. John; and there he began to develop a considerable body of work, giving hundreds of conferences and informal talks. His teaching is also developed through the means of silence, the spoken word, meditation, dances, movements, exercises, songs, etc.—thus renewing the eternal tradition of light which has been guiding humanity since the beginning of time.

He defines himself as a simple man and a technician.

All of the works and teachings that he transmits emanate from this ancestral tradition of light, which belongs to all human beings. They constitute the true roots and origins of every individual and of all peoples, and their one goal is the healthy, harmonious, free and dignified development of humanity and of the earth.

Olivier Manitara received his own training during many years of apprenticeship within the bosom of this tradition, which has remained pure in certain places on the earth. Johannite Christianity opened up to him the door to the source of all of the traditions of all peoples.

He believes that all cultures and teachings emanate from a single, unique source, and that their goal is the ennoblement of man within the light of his true being, so that he may learn how to live his passage upon the earth in a just, full, enriching and beneficial manner.

Everything that he transmits comes from a light which desires to circulate freely from one being towards another, in order to unify them within the higher concept of a Brotherhood-Sisterhood which rises above the selfishness of groups and unites men in simplicity, love, and free communal work. This teaching offers powerful, time-tested tools which allow man to improve life in every area—material as well as spiritual. Its foundation is based upon the greatest simplicity; and it has been deeply experienced and brought to life before being transmitted.

Only someone who deeply experiences all of these things himself can transmit them in a just, simple, authentic and caring way.

This book is published to help promote the free and healthy evolution of man and of the earth.

If you have felt the depth of its teachings, and if you have been touched by its message, you may wish to receive the teachings-by-correspondence written by Olivier Manitara.

These confidential booklets contain exercises, secret techniques, essences of meditations, and teachings—to help you face the difficulties of life and of the spiritual path. This is a veritable training-course, which guides the candidate inside his own temple.

These booklets have been specially conceived to awaken in man the internal processes which permit him to develop his most noble faculties and capabilities.

For any additional information, we remain entirely at your service.

Telesma-Evida Publishing
P.O. Box 174, Succ. Ahuntsic
Montreal (Qc) H3L 3N7, Canada
Email: Telesma.Publishing@Telesma-Evida.com

Visit also our Web site at
http://www.telesma-evida.com/en/publishing.htm

Other titles by Olivier Manitara

THE ESSENES

From Jesus To Our Time

Since the archaeological discovery of the Dead Sea Scrolls in 1946, the word "Essene" has made its way around the world—often raising a lot of questions. Many people were astonished to discover that, two thousand years ago, a brotherhood of holy men, living together in a community, carried within themselves all of the seeds of Christianity and of future western civilization. This brotherhood—more or less persecuted and ostracized—would bring forth people who would change the face of the world and the course of history. Indeed, almost all of the principal founders of what would later be called Christianity were Essenes—St. Ann, Joseph and Mary, John the Baptist, Jesus, John the Evangelist, etc.

CONCENTRATION
ATTENTION
AWAKENING

Their Application in Life

Concentration, attention, and the aspiration to awaken to a higher consciousness are three fundamental qualities for anyone who wishes to walk on the path towards uniting his Spirit with the Great Divine Spirit which embraces everything.

Through clear explanations which go straight to the heart of what is most essential, the author conveys a practical teaching—one which has been lived—on these three virtues which allow every person to undertake anything and to succeed in everything.

A book that is unique in its field.
A major key to a better life.

THE ROSE+CROSS

The Inner Experiences of a Student of the Current of St. John

If you wish to become a disciple of Christ, of the humanity of St. John—that is, if you wish to approach the man of light, the free, creative, good man; if you want to develop all of the gifts hidden within you and to walk on the path of enrichment, happiness, joy, success and immortality; if you aspire to the luminous and sacred knowledge of the Masters of the Solar Land of Shamballa, of the Celestial Jerusalem; and, especially, if you want to succeed fully in your life on earth—then it is for you that this book is written.

Several teachings, exercises, and initiatic methods which have remained secret for centuries are revealed in a simple way to permit the authentic seeker to progress on the path of the temple of the Rose+Cross.

This is a lived testimony, a guide and a call sent out by the contemporary Rose+Cross.

PRINTED AND BOUND
IN BOUCHERVILLE, QUÉBEC, CANADA
BY MARC VEILLEUX IMPRIMEUR INC.
IN MARCH, 1999